39,474

THE
ANCIENT
ROMANS

*W*ith special thanks to Tracy Ehrlich, Ph.D.
for her invaluable assistance in reading the manuscript.

CULTURES OF THE PAST

THE ANCIENT ROMANS

KATHRYN HINDS

BENCHMARK BOOKS

MARSHALL CAVENDISH

NEW YORK

To the teachers who made a difference:
Steve Eveleigh, Dave Moore, Mike Mellone, Jan Graeter,
Julie Greisinger, and especially Ed Downey.

*Thanks to Arthur and Owen, Mom and Dad, Jane and Dudley, Stasia and
Paul, and my editor, Judith Whipple. You all helped make this book happen,
and I couldn't have done it without you.*

Benchmark Books
Marshall Cavendish Corporation
99 White Plains Road
Tarrytown, New York 10591-9001

© Marshall Cavendish Corporation 1997

Library of Congress Cataloging-in-Publication Data

Hinds, Kathryn, date.
 The ancient Romans / by Kathryn Hinds.
  p.   cm.— (Cultures of the past)
 Includes bibliographical references and index.
 ISBN 0-7614-0090-7 (lib. bdg.)
 1. Rome—Civilization—Juvenile literature.   I. Title.   II. Series.
DG77.H5   1997
937—dc20   95-44099

SUMMARY: Traces the Roman Empire from its beginnings as a kingdom, discussing
the history, culture, deities, and legacy of the Romans.

Printed in Hong Kong

Book design by Carol Matsuyama
Photo research by Rose Corbett Gordon

Front cover: This Roman husband and wife had their picture painted together hold-
 ing a scroll and writing implements.
Back cover: Built in the first century C.E., this Roman aqueduct soars above the
 Spanish city of Segovia, still carrying water.

Photo Credits

Front cover: courtesy of SCALA/Art Resource, NY; back cover: courtesy of ©Macduff
Everton/The Image Works; page 6: Roma, Musei Capitolini, Archivio Fotografico dei
Musei Capitolini, N. 75/96 (M. Grimoldi); pages 7, 11, 15, 16, 19, 23, 25, 26, 27, 30,
32, 37, 38, 39, 43, 44–45, 47, 51, 57, 69: SCALA/Art Resource, NY; pages 8, 50, 56,
63: Erich Lessing/Art Resource, NY; page 10: North Wind Picture Archives; page 14:
Alinari/Art Resource, NY; page 17: Mike Caldwell/Tony Stone Images; page 20:
©Macduff Everton/The Image Works; page 21: ©Francis DeRichemond/The Image
Works; page 22: Werner Forman Archive/Art Resource, NY; pages 24, 68:
Giraudon/Art Resource, NY; page 28: The Metropolitan Museum of Art, The Rogers
Fund, 1903, 03.14.13; page 36: Alinari/Art Resource, NY; page 54: SCALA/Art
Resource, NY; page 55 *(top)*: Copyright The British Museum; page 55 *(bottom)*:
Tomb on the via Portuense, Museo Nationale, Rome (M. Grimoldi); page 61: The
Metropolitan Museum of Art, Purchase, 1903, 03.l4.5; page 62: Samuel H. Kress
Collection, ©1995 Board of Trustees, National Gallery of Art, Washington; page 64:
©Gianni Giansanti/Sygma; page 67: ©Vanni/Art Resource, NY; page 70: ©Michael
Melford/The Image Bank

CONTENTS

History
Chapter One   A WORLD POWER   6

Rome in the Era of the Kings   6
The Roman Republic   7
Territorial Expansion   9
Civil Strife   11
The End of the Republic   13
The Empire   16
Map   18

Cultural History
Chapter Two   PRACTICALITY AND PLEASURE   20

Buildings for Many Purposes   20
Art for All Reasons   27
Books for Past, Present, and Future   31

Belief System
Chapter Three DEITIES FOR EVERYONE   36

Divine Forces   36
Goddesses and Gods   37
Emperor Worship   41
Fortune and Fate   42
Personal Saviors   43
The Beginning of a New Order   48

Beliefs and Society
Chapter Four   THE ROMAN WAY OF LIFE   50

Patriotism and the Roman Virtues   50
Patrons and Clients   50
The Family   53
Slavery   58

The Legacy of the Romans
Chapter Five   A LASTING SOURCE OF CIVILIZATION   62

The Fate of the Empire   62
Rebirth: The Renaissance   66
The Enlightenment   71

THE ROMANS: A CHRONOLOGY   72
GLOSSARY   74
FOR FURTHER READING   76
BIBLIOGRAPHY   77
INDEX   78

CHAPTER ONE

A WORLD POWER

Julius Caesar, the most famous of ancient Romans, was a politician, conqueror, reformer, writer, and dictator. In this statue he wears the uniform of a Roman legionary soldier.

About three thousand years ago, groups of farmers and shepherds banded together to form small villages on the hills along the east bank of the Tiber River on the Italian peninsula. Eventually these villages united and grew to form one large city—Rome. This event marked the beginning of one of the most remarkable periods of human history, for from this site the Roman Empire would spread out over most of Europe and parts of Asia and Africa. The culture of the Roman people would be carried to every part of the world as they knew it, and would leave a legacy that has lasted even to today.

Rome in the Era of the Kings

According to Roman tradition, it was the legendary Romulus who founded Rome, becoming the city-state's first king, in 753 B.C.E.* He was followed by six more kings. The last three of these were Etruscan, from Etruria in north central Italy. They were responsible for beginning to truly develop the city. They established the Forum (the civic center), protective earthworks around the city, and a major temple. Rome steadily grew wealthier, less rural, and more powerful in the region.

The kings of Rome did not govern entirely alone. They were advised by a large council of elders, the Senate. This body of one hundred men (later three hundred and then six hundred) was made up of the heads of noble families. Since the members of the Senate were the *patres* (PAH-trays), "fathers," of their families, they and their descendants were called patricians (puh-TRIH-shuhns). The patricians were Rome's privileged upper class.

*Many systems of dating have been used by different cultures throughout history. This series of books uses B.C.E. (Before Common Era) and C.E. (Common Era) instead of B.C. (Before Christ) and A.D. (Anno Domini) out of respect for the diversity of the world's peoples.

The other two classes of Roman citizens were the *equites* (EH-kwee-tays) and the plebeians (pleh-BEE-uhns). The *equites* were originally knights; they were the class who could afford the equipment necessary for serving in the cavalry, although they were not as wealthy as the senators. Eventually they became Rome's banking, business, and merchant class. The plebeians were the freeborn commoners.

The Etruscans made many contributions, large and small, to Roman culture. This painting from an Etruscan tomb shows a banquet at which the diners recline on couches as they eat—a custom that was adopted by the Romans.

The Roman Republic

Around 509 B.C.E. the last king of Rome was expelled, and kingship was abolished forever. Rome became a republic governed by the Senate and the consuls, two magistrates who served for one-

Ruins of the Roman Forum. This was Rome's civic center and main meeting place. Government buildings, law courts, temples, schools, and shops surrounded a large open area where people could gather to listen to speeches, watch plays, meet their friends, or hold political demonstrations.

year terms. The consuls were elected by the Centuriate Assembly, which was a body of 193 representatives of groups organized on the basis of their ability to provide military service. Like the senators, the consuls were always patricians.

The plebeians resented the fact that they were forbidden to hold public office. They did not even have the full rights of citizenship that were enjoyed by the patricians. Around 494 B.C.E. a new office, the tribune of the plebs, was created to protect the plebeians and their interests. The tribunes also led a plebeian assembly. But it wasn't until 300 B.C.E. that the plebeians gained the right to hold any office in the republic.

THE TWELVE TABLES

One of the plebeians' complaints was that they were expected to obey laws that were known in full only by the patricians. In the years 451–449 B.C.E., in response to plebeian demands, the laws of Rome were finally codified and published as the Twelve Tables, bronze plaques that were posted in the Forum. Unfortunately, when the plebeians saw how many legal restrictions applied to them, they were far from contented. Nevertheless Rome was always extremely proud of its achievement in writing down its laws for everyone to see, and for centuries memorization of the Twelve Tables was part of every Roman boy's education.

Territorial Expansion

Meanwhile Roman power had been expanding. By 272 B.C.E. Rome was in control of the entire Italian peninsula, including the Greek settlements in the south. This conquest exposed Rome to greater Greek influence than ever before. It also brought the republic into hostile contact with what would be its archenemy, Carthage.

Carthage, the most powerful force in the Mediterranean, was a great city-state in North Africa. It had settlements in Sicily, which lay across a strait, or narrow body of water, from Rome's new territory. When Rome became involved in power struggles in Sicily, it ended up fighting the First Punic War (264–241 B.C.E.) against Carthage. Rome won, and gained not only Sicily but also the islands of Sardinia and Corsica.

Rome and Carthage were not finished with each other, however, and in 218 B.C.E. the Second Punic War began. The Carthaginian general Hannibal, with an army of forty thousand men and thirty-seven elephants, made his way from Carthage's territory in Spain and crossed the Alps into Italy. Even though Hannibal lost half his army and two-thirds of his elephants during the journey, the Romans suffered bitter defeats at his hands. One battle was so disastrous that, it was said afterward, every woman in Rome was in mourning for a dead husband, son, father, or brother. Nevertheless the Romans were determined to defeat Hannibal, and at last they were able to do so.

As the battles raged in Italy, the Roman general Scipio Africanus (SKIH-pee-oh a-frih-KA-nuhs) successfully fought the Carthaginians in Spain, gaining for Rome two new Spanish

Hannibal's invasion of Italy (shown here as a nineteenth-century artist imagined it) was one of the most traumatic events of Roman history.

provinces. When he returned to Italy, Scipio Africanus was elected consul. He immediately took an army to attack Carthage itself, and gained one of the most significant victories of history (201 B.C.E.). Defeated Carthage was deprived of its power, and for hundreds of years afterward, Rome controlled the Mediterranean.

In 200 B.C.E. Rome went to war against Macedonia (ma-suh-DOH-nee-uh), in what is now northern Greece, beginning a series of conquests in the eastern Mediterranean. Macedonia fell to Rome in 168 B.C.E. In 146 B.C.E. the Romans abolished the Achaean (uh-KEE-uhn) League of Greek city-states; burned its capital, Corinth, to the ground; and annexed Greece. The Third Punic War came to its climax with Rome's total destruction of the city of Carthage the same year. By 129 B.C.E. the republic had also gained control of much of Asia Minor.

In 312 B.C.E. the Romans built the first of their great roads, the Appian (A-pee-uhn) Way, during a war with the Samnites, a tribe of central Italy. The Samnites had twice as many people and twice as much territory as the Romans. Yet the Romans were victorious, largely because the Appian Way allowed troops and supplies to reach the battlefields with such great ease.

From then on Rome's territorial expansion was always accompanied by highway construction. On the Italian peninsula the state paid for the roads, but in the provinces the costs were borne by local communities. Roman engineers oversaw the construction; the actual work was frequently done by soldiers between military campaigns. These roads were so well built that they could often last a hundred years without needing any repairs, and some sections even remained in use into modern times.

Eventually there were fifty thousand miles of roads, systematically distributed throughout the Roman world, all of them ultimately leading to Rome. Although they were built mainly for military purposes, they were used by merchants and other civilian travelers as well. The network of highways ensured excellent communications between the capital and the provinces and helped Rome to become one of the most well organized states in history.

The Appian Way was the first of the great Roman roads. Outside the city, it was lined on either side with the splendid tombs of wealthy Roman families.

Civil Strife

The Roman Republic now ruled an empire that spanned three continents. But there were serious troubles at home in Italy. After the Second Punic War, traditional small family farms began to be replaced by huge sheep and cattle ranches and by plantations that produced profitable cash crops such as olives and grapes. Wealthy landowners grew even wealthier by using slave labor to work these large estates, so there was no work for the freeborn poor in the country. Many of these people moved to the city, where they seldom found jobs and were easily whipped up into riots. To add to the problem, this growing population of landless poor could not be called on to serve in the army, because Roman soldiers had to own a certain amount of property. It was clear that reforms were necessary.

In 133 B.C.E. Tiberius Sempronius Gracchus (ty-BEER-ee-uhs sehm-PROH-nee-uhs GRA-kuhs) became tribune. He created a program, which was approved by the Assembly, to give allotments of government-owned land to the urban poor and to reduce the amount of land held by the wealthy. This plan seemed extremely radical to many in the Senate. When Tiberius attempted to run for reelection, he and three hundred of his supporters were clubbed to death by a group of senators and their allies.

In 123 and again in 122 B.C.E., Tiberius's brother Gaius (GUY-uhs) held the tribuneship. Gaius reintroduced Tiberius's land-reform program; he also planned to establish new colonies, where the poor could settle, in southern Italy and on the site of Carthage; and he arranged for the monthly distribution of grain at a reduced price. In addition he tried to lessen the power of the Senate by giving new privileges to the *equites*. When Gaius lost his bid for a third term as tribune, fighting broke out. The Senate declared a state of emergency, during which Gaius was killed by a crowd led by one of the consuls. Soon afterward three thousand of his supporters were executed.

Victories and Crises

Meanwhile Rome was gaining new territory in what is now France. Then, from 112 to 105 B.C.E., the republic waged a victorious war against Numidia (modern-day Algeria), enlarging its African holdings. The hero of this war was the ambitious general Marius, who gained further glory by destroying two forces of mingled Celtic (KEL-tik) and Germanic tribes that had been rampaging through Roman territory.

To increase the size of his army, Marius had ignored the property requirements for military service, and thousands of landless volunteers joined up. These soldiers were fiercely devoted to Marius, and he rewarded them by settling them in colonies in the conquered territories. Although Marius's new kind of army was highly effective, it set a fateful precedent: From then on, Roman armies were more loyal to their commander than to their country.

The next crisis was the Social War (91–87 B.C.E.), in which many of the Italian city-states that were subject to Rome declared war against the republic. In some cases they were fighting for full

Roman citizenship and in others for complete independence. The war laid waste to the countryside. It finally ended with Rome granting citizenship to all Italian communities south of the Po River. But now that the majority of Roman citizens lived too far from the capital to take part in its regular political life, the old republican city-state government became increasingly outmoded.

At the same time, trouble was brewing in the eastern Mediterranean, where King Mithradates VI (MIH-thruh-DAY-tees) of Pontus (now northern Turkey) was attempting to overthrow Roman rule in Asia Minor and Greece. The command against Mithradates was first given to Lucius Cornelius Sulla (LOO-shuhs cor-NEEL-yuhs SUH-luh) but then handed instead to Marius. Sulla refused to step down, led his troops into Rome, and assumed the consulship in 88 B.C.E. He then went to war against Mithradates, driving him out of Greece but allowing him to continue ruling in Asia Minor as an ally of Rome.

The Roman government was now in the hands of Sulla's political enemies, who outlawed him. Sulla and his army invaded Rome and massacred the city's defenders. He had more than ten thousand of his opponents executed, confiscating their land and distributing it to his soldiers. In 81 B.C.E. Sulla declared himself dictator for the purpose of "making laws and setting up the state." His dictatorship was peaceful and introduced many reforms. In 80 B.C.E. Sulla became consul, and the next year he retired. Ultimately, however, his reconstruction of the government could not save the republic.

The End of the Republic

In the next decade two new energetic, ambitious military leaders arose—Pompey (PAHM-pee) and Crassus (KRA-suhs). They joined forces and in 70 B.C.E. became consuls, over the Senate's objection, even though neither one of them was legally qualified. In 66 B.C.E. Pompey wiped out the pirates that were disrupting trade in the eastern Mediterranean, and the next year he put an end to Mithradates's rule in Asia Minor. He went on to conquer Syria and to bring Judaea (joo-DEE-uh), today southern Israel, under Roman control.

The great orator Cicero was what was called a "new man"—none of his ancestors had ever held office. But because of his brilliant public speaking, Cicero was able to become one of Rome's leading citizens.

In 63 B.C.E. a nobleman named Catiline (KA-tuh-line) plotted to attack Rome with a private army and seize power for himself. The conspiracy was discovered and ended by the great orator Cicero (SIH-suh-roh), who was consul at the time. However, when Cicero ordered the execution of some of Catiline's co-conspirators without a trial, another rising politician opposed him. This was Julius Caesar. Caesar's protest was unsuccessful, but he gained many powerful allies.

During the next few years, the Senate seriously insulted Pompey, Crassus, and Caesar. The three men therefore joined together in 60 B.C.E. to form a secret political group known as the First Triumvirate (try-UHM-vuh-ruht). Caesar invited Cicero to join, too, but the orator was a staunch believer in republican institutions and refused the offer.

The First Triumvirate quickly wrested the government of Rome away from the Senate, arranging for Caesar to be consul in 59 B.C.E. The following year Caesar began the conquest of Gaul (modern-day France, Belgium, and parts of Germany), an undertaking that lasted until 51 B.C.E. Meanwhile Pompey remained in Rome to keep things under control there. Crassus attempted to conquer the Parthians, of what is now Iran, but was defeated and killed in 53 B.C.E.

From that time on, tensions grew between Pompey and Caesar. Caesar returned to Italy at the head of his army in 49 B.C.E., quickly gaining command of the entire peninsula. Pompey fled the country, eventually landing in Egypt, where he was murdered. Caesar pursued him there and began a relationship with Queen Cleopatra VII. With Caesar's help Cleopatra defeated her political enemies and became the undisputed ruler of Egypt. During the next few years Caesar put down rebellions in various parts of the Roman world, which he now completely controlled.

When Caesar went back to the capital, he set up new colonies for his soldiers and the unemployed, and made great strides in handling Rome's serious debt problem. He also had many splendid buildings erected. He had held the office of dictator since 49 B.C.E., and in February of 44 B.C.E. was appointed dictator for the rest of his life. The next month, as he prepared to head east on another war of conquest, Caesar was stabbed to death by a group of senators who saw him as the destroyer of the republic.

In 43 B.C.E. the government was taken over by the Second Triumvirate, whose members were Caesar's nineteen-year-old adopted son, Octavius (ahk-TAY-vee-uhs); Caesar's right-hand man, Mark Antony; and another of Caesar's aides, Lepidus (LEH-pih-dus). One of the dictators' first acts was to arrange the murders of their political opponents, including two thousand *equites* and three hundred senators, among them Cicero. Octavius controlled most of Rome's western provinces, and Antony most of the eastern provinces.

Relations between Antony and Octavius were always rather strained, but they worsened when Antony's wife, Fulvia (FUHL-

Octavius defeated Antony and Cleopatra with warships like these. The oars were manned by slaves or criminals.

vee-uh), and his brother joined in a rebellion against Octavius. Fulvia died soon afterward, and Antony patched things up with Octavius by marrying his sister, Octavia. Before long, however, Antony deserted Octavia and Rome in favor of Cleopatra and Egypt. Octavius declared war on Cleopatra and won a decisive naval battle against her and Antony in 31 B.C.E. The two defeated leaders committed suicide, and Octavius annexed Egypt as a province under his personal control. Since Lepidus had been forced into retirement several years earlier, Octavius was left as the sole ruler of the Roman Empire.

Augustus led Rome out of the chaos of the end of the republic and remolded the Roman state so well that it lasted hundreds of years more.

The Empire

Octavius's main concern now was to restore peace and stability to Rome. Although he kept all real political power in his own hands, he carefully maintained the outward forms of the old republican government. He did not call himself emperor but instead took titles meaning "first citizen" and "father of the country." From 27 B.C.E. onward, he was known as Augustus, a name associated with religion and authority.

During his long rule Augustus gave the Senate new administrative functions, assigned important roles to the *equites,* reduced the size of the army, and started a civil service. He extended the empire to its northernmost boundary, the Danube River. He introduced legislation that promoted traditional Roman family and religious values. He restored many old temples, and under his reign literature, sculpture, and architecture flourished.

Because of Augustus and the stable form of government he created, Rome was able to survive for centuries more. New conquests continued to expand the empire to almost the edges of the known world. Throughout the empire, diverse ethnic and religious groups lived mostly in peace with one another, and the number of people who enjoyed a comfortable middle-class lifestyle was larger than ever before.

None of the emperors who followed Augustus were quite so gifted as he was, but many of them came close. Outstanding among

these were Trajan (TRAY-juhn), Hadrian (HAY-dree-uhn), Antoni- nus Pius (an-tuh-NY-nuhs PY-us), and the philosopher-emperor Marcus Aurelius (aw-REEL-yuhs), all of whom ruled during the second century C.E.

In the reign of Marcus Aurelius, however, German tribes came swarming over the Danube. Aurelius was able to deal with the situation effectively, but from then on attacks on the empire's borders became almost constant. Later emperors had to pour ever more money into maintaining the army, with the result that the middle class was practically taxed out of existence. For the same

The farthest outpost of Roman rule was Britain, conquered between 43 and 84 C.E. Around 121 C.E. the emperor Hadrian visited the island and directed the building of a great wall to protect Roman settlements against raiding tribes from the area of what is now Scotland. Remains of Hadrian's Wall can still be seen across much of northern Britain.

17

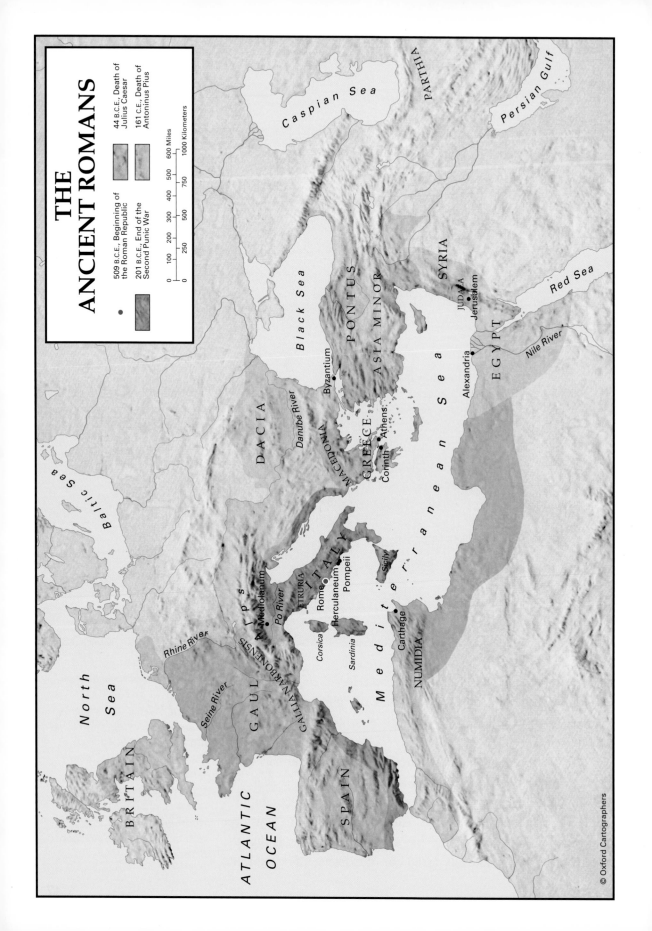

THE
ANCIENT ROMANS

509 B.C.E., Beginning of the Roman Republic

201 B.C.E., End of the Second Punic War

• 44 B.C.E., Death of Julius Caesar

161 C.E., Death of Antoninus Pius

0 100 200 300 400 500 600 Miles
0 250 500 750 1000 Kilometers

Caspian Sea

PARTHIA

Persian Gulf

Black Sea

PONTUS

ASIA MINOR

SYRIA

JUDAEA
Jerusalem

Red Sea

Alexandria

EGYPT

Nile River

Baltic Sea

DACIA

Danube River

MACEDONIA

GREECE
Athens
Corinth

Mediterranean Sea

North Sea

Rhine River

GAUL

Seine River

GALLIA NARBONENSIS

Alps

Mediolanum

Po River

ETRURIA

ITALY

Rome
Herculaneum
Pompeii

Sicily

Corsica

Sardinia

Carthage

NUMIDIA

ATLANTIC OCEAN

BRITAIN

SPAIN

Byzantium

© Oxford Cartographers

The Romans called the German tribes, along with other peoples who did not speak Latin or Greek, barbarians. In art, barbarian men were usually shown wearing caps, trousers, and beards. Here the victorious Romans are enslaving and executing barbarian prisoners.

reason, large numbers of the rural poor were either driven underground into lives as roving bandits or forced to become the serfs of wealthy landowners.

The empire grew extremely difficult to rule, especially from Rome, which was too far down the Italian peninsula for the emperor to keep an eye on the unstable borders. In 330 C.E. Emperor Constantine I (KAHN-stuhn-teen) established the city of Constantinople (KAHN-stan-tih-NOH-puhl)—at what is now Istanbul, Turkey—as his capital. This move permanently changed the empire's center of gravity from the west to the east. Moreover, Constantine made Christianity the empire's official religion. These two developments marked a definitive break with the past, although the Roman Empire continued to survive as a political entity for roughly another 150 years.

CHAPTER TWO

PRACTICALITY AND PLEASURE

*Others will more pleasingly mold bronze to seem it breathes
(I truly believe), will form living faces from marble;
will better plead their causes; will describe and point out
the motion of the heavens and name the rising constellations.
You, Roman, be mindful to lead the nations by your power
(these arts are yours) and to establish the rule of peace,
to spare those who are cast down, and to vanquish the proud.*
                        —*Aeneid* (author's translation)

A s this passage by the great Roman poet Virgil shows, the Romans thought of themselves as being more talented in the art of government than in anything else. In fact most Roman architecture, sculpture, and painting was produced by non-Italians, mainly Greeks. However, these artists worked under the enthusiastic patronage of wealthy and important Romans, and remolded older cultural traditions to suit Roman needs and taste.

Buildings for Many Purposes

Ancient Rome has always been famous for its great achievements in architecture and engineering. These feats were accomplished largely thanks to the Roman invention of concrete, which could bear greater weight than stone. Concrete structures were usually covered with plaster, brick, or even such expensive materials as bronze, marble, and alabaster.

The emperor Hadrian was a devoted patron of the arts and was himself skilled in music, painting, architecture, and mathematics. This is a portion of the beautiful grounds of Hadrian's Villa near Tivoli, Italy, which was a popular health resort in Roman times.

The Pont du Gard near Nîmes in southern France was built during the reign of Augustus. It is one of the best-preserved and most spectacular of Roman aqueducts still standing.

The most distinctive element of Roman architecture was probably the arch, which was originally brought to Rome by the Etruscans. Arches were used in all sorts of structures. Bridges were typically supported by a series of large arches, as were the above-ground portions of aqueducts (A-kwuh-duhkts), which might even have two or three tiers, or levels, of arches.

For the Love of Running Water

A Roman aqueduct was a masonry channel that carried water over a long distance to supply a city. The water flowed into reservoirs, and from there lead pipes conveyed it throughout the community. Drains and sewers carried away wastewater.

By the year 109 C.E. Rome was served by eleven aqueducts. Romans were very proud of their aqueducts and pointed them out as evidence of the empire's greatness, bragging that aqueducts were much more useful than such monuments as Egypt's pyramids. In fact Roman cities did have marvelous water supplies. Some wealthy people had indoor plumbing, but most of the water was intended for use by the general public. Every city block had a fountain where people could obtain water for drinking, cooking, and washing. There were huge public baths and conveniently located public lavatories with continuously flushing toilets.

Hot rooms of a bathhouse near Pompeii's forum. The walls are hollow to allow hot air to circulate from furnaces under the floor.

A ROMAN BATH

From the late republic onward, bathing was an important part of a Roman's daily routine. Every afternoon before dinner, people would go to the great public bathhouses, which were open to everyone who could pay the small entrance fee. At one point there were more than eight hundred bathhouses in Rome alone. Many of them were splendid buildings, decorated with colored marble and works of art. Bathhouses had separate accommodations for women and for men.

A full Roman bath was an elaborate affair. Bathers undressed in a changing room that contained compartments for storing clothes. Then they went into a warm room called a *tepidarium* (TEH-pih-DA-ree-uhm), where they stayed until they began to perspire. The next room was the *caldarium* (kal-DA-ree-uhm), a hot room. Here they had a hot bath. They could also go into another hot room, the *laconicum* (la-KAH-nih-kuhm), which was like a sauna. Before moving on to the *frigidarium* (frih-gih-DA-ree-uhm) for a cold bath, they used a metal scraper to remove perspiration. Finally bathers passed into the *unctorium* (unk-TOH-ree-uhm) to be massaged and rubbed with oil. Bathers provided their own scrapers, linen towels, and oil.

Large bathhouses had facilities for exercising and socializing as well as for washing. Many had gymnasiums, exercise grounds, ball courts, and swimming pools. There might also be libraries, reading rooms, and rooms for gaming and conversation. Vendors and snack bars sold food and drink to bathers. For the Romans a bath was as much a form of recreation as a way to get clean.

For the Love of Spectacle

Another kind of structure in which arches played a major role was the amphitheater (AM-fuh-thee-uh-ter), a huge oval building. In its center was a large, flat, open space called an arena, which was

The Flavian Amphitheater, now known as the Colosseum, opened in 80 C.E. Beneath the arena was a huge network of underground passages, rooms, and cells for the humans and animals who took part in the amphitheater's bloody spectacles.

surrounded by tiers of seats. The outside walls of amphitheaters built during the first centuries of the Common Era generally featured concrete arcades—rows of arches—stacked one on top of another to a height of up to four stories. One of the most famous and best-preserved of the surviving Roman buildings, the Colosseum, was an amphitheater. It could accommodate fifty thousand people.

Roman amphitheaters were such magnificent architectural achievements that it can be hard to believe they were erected to house the bloodiest spectator sports ever known. In the amphitheater, pairs of specially trained professional fighters called gladiators (GLA-dee-ay-tors) battled, often to the death. Gladiatorial contests were immensely popular from the late republic onward. They were paid for by wealthy citizens, candidates for office, government officials, or emperors in order to win over the masses. The sports of the arena distracted people from their troubles—especially the large numbers of unemployed, who were prone to rioting.

But the populace demanded ever larger, bloodier, more spectacular entertainments. Recently won battles were reenacted. The arena was flooded so that naval combats could be staged. Wild animals were brought in to kill one another or to be hunted. Sometimes

gladiators fought the animals, and sometimes unarmed people (slaves or condemned prisoners) were thrown to the animals to be torn apart and devoured.

Even more popular—and somewhat less violent—than the entertainments of the amphitheater were those that took place in buildings called circuses. There were six circuses in and around the city of Rome alone. The largest of these had seats for 60,000 people in the time of Augustus and was later enlarged to accommodate over 200,000. The games held in the circus were paid for by the same people, for the same reasons, as those put on in the amphitheater.

The circus had a long, rather narrow, oval arena with a barrier down most of the middle. The shows here were mainly exhibitions of horsemanship of one kind or another. Most crowd-pleasing of all were chariot races. Light chariots, pulled usually by four horses, ran seven laps around the barrier. The course was relatively short and the turns were sharp, so these races could be quite dangerous for horses and drivers. Indeed it was not the speed of the race but the danger that thrilled the spectators. Successful drivers, even though they were often slaves, became wealthy celebrities.

For the Love of the Deities

Augustus sponsored numerous free entertainments to help keep himself in favor with the people. To help keep Rome in favor with the deities, he sponsored the repair of many old temples and the building of many new ones. Most Roman temples were like Greek temples: rectangular, fronted by large columned porches, with triangular peaked roofs. Some Roman temples, most notably the temple of Hercules near the Forum, were round.

But the most famous Roman temple of all, the Pantheon, was very different from all the others. It was given its distinctive form by the emperor Hadrian. Behind the usual porch with its columns, the Pan-theon was roofed with a magnificent concrete dome, the like of which had never before been erected. The dome had a twenty-seven-foot-wide circular opening in the center to let in light, so that few portions of the interior were ever in shadow. The dome represented heaven, and the central opening symbolized the sun—this temple was dedicated to the worship of all the deities, but especially those connected with the stars and planets.

The Pantheon was built during the reign of Augustus and then completely renovated under the direction of Hadrian.

For the Love of Home

The first Romans lived in round, one-roomed houses with thatched roofs. Even in the time of Augustus there were still poor people living in such homes on one of the hills of Rome, and the majority of people in rural areas probably had similar dwellings.

Most residents of Rome and other cities lived in apartment buildings, called *insulae* (IHN-soo-lye). The use of concrete for their walls enabled the *insulae* to rise as high as seven stories. They

The remains of the atrium of a house in Herculaneum, Italy. The impluvium *can be seen in the middle; to the back is the wide entrance to the* tablinum. *Herculaneum and neighboring Pompeii were destroyed by the eruption of Mount Vesuvius in 79 C.E. The covering of volcanic ash preserved these two Roman cities almost intact, and they were discovered in the eighteenth century.*

were usually built around a central courtyard. The ground floors were taken up by shops. Some apartments had several rooms, but it seems that most had just one. The only light came through windows overlooking the street or the courtyard, so inner rooms were always dark.

Wealthy Romans had impressive private homes. The first room in such a house was the atrium (AY-tree-uhm), which was sometimes separated from the door to the street by a short hallway. The atrium was originally the part of the house where the family spent most of its time. Toward the end of the republic, though, it became a room used only for formal occasions and for receiving visitors. The main features of the atrium were the *compluvium* (kuhm-PLOO-vee-uhm), a rectangular or square opening in the roof, and below it the *impluvium* (ihm-PLOO-vee-uhm), a pool

built into the floor. The *compluvium* admitted not only light but also rainwater, which filled the *impluvium* and from there ran into a cistern, or tank, thus providing the house's main water supply.

On each side of the atrium were one to three rooms and, at the back, an open alcove. Behind the atrium, directly opposite the front door, was a wide room called the *tablinum* (TA-blih-nuhm), which could be closed off from the rest of the house with curtains or folding doors. The *tablinum* was the office or study of the father of the family.

In back of the *tablinum* was the peristyle, a courtyard surrounded by a paved walkway that was covered with a roof supported by columns. Various rooms opened off the walkway, among them bedrooms, the kitchen, dining rooms, storerooms, slave quarters, a library, toilets, and perhaps bathing facilities and even stables. When a house had two stories, the bedrooms were often upstairs. The peristyle customarily had a fountain or pool, decorative statues, and an elaborate garden.

Art for All Reasons

The homes of wealthy Romans were beautifully adorned with all sorts of artwork. Walls were painted with large rectangles in rich colors or with mythological scenes, still lifes, landscapes, or architectural vistas. Such wall paintings are called frescoes (FREHS-kohs), meaning "fresh," because they were painted when the plaster of the wall was still wet. Ceilings, too, were painted, or ornamented with carved beams or with reliefs in stucco (a kind of plaster).

Cave canem (KAH-vay KAH-nehm) is Latin for "beware of the dog." This mosaic is from the entrance of a house in Pompeii.

Floors were decorated with mosaics (moh-ZAY-ihks), tiny pieces of colored tile laid together to form a design or picture. Mosaics could depict flowers, animals, hunting scenes, magical symbols, and even such large subjects as historic battles—in fact, just about anything. A very popular mosaic design, used in the entrances of many Roman homes, was a picture of a large dog—the ancient equivalent of a BEWARE OF THE DOG sign.

The mosaic floor and frescoed walls of this room from a Roman villa (country house) of around 40 C.E. show how elaborately the homes of wealthy Romans were decorated.

Statues were also used to decorate the homes of the rich; many of these statues were copies of Greek works. But sculpture had other functions besides its ornamental one. Perhaps its earliest major use was in temples, which usually contained statues of the deities honored in them, giving worshipers a focus for their prayers.

Images of goddesses and gods were carved according to classical Greek ideals of form and beauty, since these works of art were supposed to be representations of divine perfection. Portrait statues of human beings, which were in great demand from the last century of the republic onward, sometimes followed the same ideal. More often, though, the Romans preferred their portraits to be realistic, not even leaving out physical flaws. This attitude resulted from the Romans' growing emphasis on the needs and concerns of the individual and from the belief that the face was the mirror of the soul. Portraits, then, were expected to express the unique personality of the person portrayed.

MASKS OF THE ANCESTORS

Roman interest in portrait sculpture had a long social history. From early times patrician families had kept wax death masks (molded over the features of the dead person) of all their ancestors who had held high office. These masks were arranged as a family tree in a special cabinet in one of the wings off the atrium. The cabinet was probably opened frequently so that children could be taught about the deeds of their ancestors. At family funerals actors were hired to wear the masks in the funeral procession.

The most important portraits sculpted for the Romans were those of the emperors. Every emperor felt that it was essential for his subjects to know what he looked like. Without newspapers or television, the best way to do this was through sculpture and the portraits that appeared on coins. Full-length statues as well as busts (sculptures of a person's head and shoulders) were sent out to all parts of the empire. A single emperor's portraits might project a number of different images, some of them chosen to suit specific parts of the empire: the great conqueror, the divine ruler,

THE ANCIENT ROMANS

the democratic statesman, the philosophical thinker, the bearer of the burdens of government, the common man.

Relief sculpture, which adorned temples and other buildings, was also used on all sorts of monuments by emperors in order to build or keep up their reputations. The reliefs on Augustus's Altar of Peace show mythological scenes and a religious procession in which the emperor and his family are taking part. The Arch of Titus has reliefs depicting that emperor's triumphal return from his conquest of Jerusalem. The Column of Trajan is sculpted with a band of reliefs spiraling up its length, picturing Trajan's war against the Dacians (a people of what is now Romania). Such reliefs ensured the lasting fame of an emperor's deeds.

On Augustus's Altar of Peace in Rome members of his court and family take part in a religious procession. The fidgeting children give the formal scene a warmth and humanity that must have appealed to Augustus's subjects as much as they do to modern viewers of this monument.

WHITE OR BRIGHT?

Although some Roman sculpture was produced in terracotta (baked clay) and bronze, marble was the most prominent material. Today when we see Roman statues and reliefs in museums, they are usually gleaming white. But on closer inspection, some may show traces of paint, for in Roman times much marble sculpture was in fact brightly colored.

Books for Past, Present, and Future

In literature as in all the other arts, the Romans were deeply influenced by the Greeks. But Roman authors (many of whom were actually from Spain, Gaul, or North Africa) wrote in the Roman language, Latin, and used their Greek inspiration to create something entirely their own. The Romans, it turned out, excelled in literature as well as in government.

The first major works of Roman literature were the plays of Plautus (PLAW-tuhs). These were all high-spirited slapstick comedies and remained extremely popular with Romans for centuries after Plautus's death in 184 B.C.E. Plautus was followed by another comic playwright, Terence (c. 186–159 B.C.E.), whose plays were less rowdy and always featured a sentimental pair of young lovers. In both authors' comedies, much of the dialogue was recited to a musical accompaniment or was actually sung while the actors danced.

The Age of Cicero

A century after Plautus and Terence, Roman literature came into full flower. The foremost literary figure of this time was Cicero (106–43 B.C.E.). A vast amount of Cicero's work has survived to the present, including many personal letters and philosophical essays as well as his famous speeches. With his wit and his masterful use of words, Cicero made public speaking an art form. His elegant and complex style was the model for nearly all Latin prose writing that

This first-century C.E. mosaic from Pompeii shows actors preparing for a performance. On the right and at the bottom center are the masks they will wear. The third actor from the left is costumed as a woman; he is playing a double flute.

followed, and his interpretations of Greek philosophy were equally influential.

Cicero's fellow senator Julius Caesar (100–44 B.C.E.) not only made history but also wrote it. His book about his conquest of Gaul, *The Gallic War,* has been admired for its clear, precise, objective style and has been read with great interest ever since it was composed. Caesar's *Civil War,* about the events leading up to his becoming dictator, has also continued to hold people's interest through the centuries.

The time of Cicero and Caesar was also the time of the first great Latin poetry. The young poet Catullus (kuh-TUH-luhs) (c. 84–54 B.C.E.) wrote brilliantly on a range of subjects. His most famous poems, though, describe with emotional intensity the exalted joys and deep sorrows of an ill-fated love affair. Another kind of poetry altogether was composed by Lucretius (loo-KREE-shuhs)

ROMAN THEATER

Like gladiatorial contests and chariot races, plays were presented free to the public on holidays. (Unfortunately, audiences would often get up and leave in the middle of a play if they heard of a more exciting event taking place at the same time.) Plays were put on in the afternoon or morning. All of the actors were male slaves. In the early days of Roman theater they wore simple Greek costumes and a little makeup. Later they wore masks and wigs that indicated the sort of characters they were playing.

In the time of Plautus and Terence, plays were given in temporary wooden theaters that were pulled down as soon as the holiday celebration ended. The first permanent theater in Rome was built of stone by Pompey in 55 B.C.E. The opening performances featured huge spectacles, including scenes in which real cavalry and infantry troops, accompanied by hundreds of mules loaded with plunder, acted out the looting of a conquered city. This was the sort of theatrical performance that increasingly attracted later Roman audiences.

(c. 96–55 B.C.E.). In his book-length philosophical poem *De rerum natura* (day RAY-rum nah-TOO-ruh), *On the Nature of Things,* he painted vivid and original word pictures of his vision of the nature of the universe.

The Golden Age

Under Augustus, Rome enjoyed a literary golden age and produced some of the greatest poets the world has ever known. Chief among these was Virgil (70–19 B.C.E.). Virgil's early works celebrated traditional rural life but also worked in myths, romance, and reflections on the human condition. His masterpiece, not quite completed when he died, was the *Aeneid* (ih-NEE-ihd).

The *Aeneid* tells the story of Aeneas (ih-NEE-uhs), a Trojan warrior, son of the goddess Venus. When the Greeks conquer Troy, Aeneas and a few others manage to escape the burning city. After much wandering around the Mediterranean, Aeneas and his companions land at Carthage, where Aeneas and the queen of that city, Dido (DY-do), fall in love. Aeneas is strongly tempted to remain with Dido in Carthage, but the supreme god Jupiter sends a messenger to remind him that his destiny is to found a new kingdom in Italy. Aeneas obediently but reluctantly leaves Dido, who kills herself out of grief. In southern Italy Aeneas meets a woman prophet called the Sibyl, who guides him to the underworld. Here Aeneas talks with the spirit of his recently deceased father, who foretells Rome's future greatness. Aeneas also encounters the spirit of Dido, who turns away and refuses to speak to him. When Aeneas finally comes near the site of Rome, he is welcomed by King Latinus, who offers his daughter Lavinia to be Aeneas's wife. But other Italian kings are not so welcoming, and Aeneas fights many battles in order to secure his place. At last he is victorious, and he and Lavinia can wed and become the ancestors of the Romans.

The *Aeneid* is full of romance and adventure—and patriotism. Virgil had lived through the civil strife of the end of the republic and was happy to celebrate the peace and stability that Augustus had brought to Rome. The historian Livy (59 B.C.E.–17 C.E.) shared this viewpoint. Throughout his history of Rome, from its founding to his own day, Livy glorified the unique destiny of the Romans. Another patriotic writer was Horace (65–8 B.C.E.), who had a gift for phrasing everyday, commonsense ideas perfectly. He composed poems for official occasions as well as love poems, satirical poems, letters in verse, and a famous verse essay on the nature of literature.

Unlike Virgil, Horace, and Livy, the poet Ovid (43 B.C.E.–17 C.E.) did not enjoy the favor of Augustus. Witty and irreverent, Ovid's poems often disregarded the traditional values that Augustus promoted. But Ovid was a supreme storyteller with a keen understanding of human emotions, and at least two of his surviving works have always been regarded as masterpieces. The *Heroides* (huh-ROH-ih-deez) is a collection of letters from legendary women to their husbands and lovers. The *Metamorphoses* (meh-tuh-MOR-fuh-seez), *Transformations,* brings together a great number of Greek and Roman myths, both major and minor. Like Virgil's *Aeneid,* it has long been one of the most popular and influential books in the Western world.

The Silver Age

The "silver age" of Latin literature produced less great poetry, but there were other important works. Seneca (died 65 C.E.) wrote the only Roman tragic dramas that have survived to the present, as well as many philosophical essays. Satire was a popular type of litera-ture at this time: Petronius (died 66 C.E.) composed a satirical novel, and Juvenal (died 127 C.E.) wrote satirical poems that viciously attacked everything that he felt was wrong with Rome. The notable historians of the silver age were Tacitus (c. 56–c. 120 C.E.), today regarded as the greatest Roman writer of history, and Suetonius (soo-eh-TOH-nee-uhs) (c. 69–after 122 C.E.), who com-posed gossipy biographies of the first twelve emperors.

One of the best-loved works of Latin literature is the *Metamorphoses* or *Golden Ass* of Apuleius (a-poo-LAY-uhs) (c. 124–after 170 C.E.). This novel tells the adventures of Lucius (LOO-shuhs), who becomes overly curious about magic and acci-dentally transforms himself into an ass (donkey). He retains his human abilities of perception and thinking, but cannot speak. Robbers carry him off, and in their hideout he hears the beautiful story of Cupid, the god of love, and Psyche (SY-kee), the maiden Cupid secretly marries. Psyche, "Soul," is forbidden to see her husband's face, but her curiosity gets the better of her and she lights a lamp at night to look at him. Cupid flies away, and Psyche must perform many difficult tasks, even entering the underworld, before she can finally be reunited with him. Like Psyche, Lucius undergoes great hardships. At last he nearly despairs of ever regaining his human form. Then, on the seashore, the goddess Isis (I-sihs) appears to him and promises her help. The next day a priest of Isis turns him back into a man, and Lucius joyfully devotes the rest of his life to serving the merciful goddess who has raised up his fallen soul.

CHAPTER THREE

DEITIES FOR EVERYONE

The Roman Empire was one of the most multicultural states in the history of the world. Just as it included a large number of ethnic groups, it also included a wide range of religious beliefs and practices. All types of religious feeling and experience could be found in ancient Rome, and all were tolerated so long as they were not perceived as dangerous or threatening to the state. Individuals therefore had a wide range of choices to satisfy their spiritual needs.

A household shrine to the Lares and the father's genius. The Lares are depicted as dancing young men, and the father's genius is represented by the snake. In the center is the father himself.

Divine Forces

In early Roman times the focus of religion was on the home, the farm, and the family. It did not center on goddesses and gods but on impersonal powers or spirits called numina (NOO-mih-nuh). A numen (the singular form of *numina*) was the divine force that was present in a specific activity, such as plowing a field, giving birth to a child, learning to talk, or even simply eating or opening a door. Places—for example, the storeroom, the threshold, and the boundary stone— also had numina. Natural features of the landscape were likewise believed to be inhabited by spirits—the more beautiful or impressive the feature, the more powerful the spirit.

Closely related to the numina were the Lares (LAH-rays), which were the family guardians. Every home had a shrine dedicated to the Lares, and the family made offerings of food and wine to them at every meal. Honored along with the Lares was the genius, or guardian spirit, of the father of the family. Every male had his own genius; a female's guardian was her *juno* (JOO-noh). The manes (MAH-nays), spirits of the dead, also played an important role in the family religion.

They were honored at their tombs during an annual festival. The Lares, genius, *juno*, and manes were worshiped from early Roman times until the empire became Christian.

Statues of Vestal Virgins in the Roman Forum

Goddesses and Gods

Because the numina were not thought of as having human appearances or personalities, there were no statues made of them and no myths (stories) told about them. However, after coming into contact with the Etruscans and especially the Greeks, the Romans began to think of divine power in terms of humanlike goddesses and gods, just as those peoples did. Many of the numina became deities of this type, among them Janus (JA-nuhs), god of beginnings, who was originally the numen of the doorway; and Venus (VEE-nuhs), goddess of love, who was originally a numen of the garden.

When the Romans saw similarities between their native spirits and the deities of the Greeks, they took over the Greek myths for their own deities. For example Venus was identified with the Greek goddess Aphrodite (a-froh-DY-tee), so the Romans told the same stories about Venus that the Greeks told about Aphrodite. The Romans also began to put statues of these divine beings in temples dedicated to their worship.

One of the most important old numina was Vesta, the spirit of the hearth. She now became one of the most important deities, although still no statues were ever made of her or stories told about her. She continued to preside over the hearth in every home, and a temple was built to her in the Roman Forum. Here her sacred fire burned continually, tended by six priestesses called Vestal Virgins. These were women from respected families who served in the temple for a minimum of thirty years, beginning when they were between six and ten years old. They were the most privileged and honored women in Rome, for it was believed that the welfare of the state depended on their carrying out the sacred duties of the hearth.

The supreme god of ancient Rome was Jupiter, "god the father," called the Best and Greatest. He was the god of the sky and

Jupiter, god of the sky and supreme god of the Roman state. He holds a thunderbolt and a staff crowned with an eagle, the symbol of Rome.

the guardian of the Roman state and its laws. Jupiter's wife was Juno, who watched over all women, particularly in marriage and during childbirth. She stood for youthfulness and strength, and was also associated with light.

A major Etruscan deity who was taken over by the Romans was Minerva (mih-NER-vuh), goddess of wisdom and of the arts and crafts. She also had a warlike aspect. Jupiter, Juno, and Minerva

Juno began as the spirit and guardian of womanhood and became queen of the deities.

39

AUGURY AND PORTENTS

A group of Roman priests called the augurs specialized in finding out what the deities, especially Jupiter, wanted people to do. Before any important public or private event, an animal was ritually slaughtered (to be eaten later), and the augurs examined its internal organs, particularly the liver. The condition of the organs told the augurs whether or not the deities approved of the action that was about to be taken.

By the first century B.C.E., few people took augury seriously. However, many still wholeheartedly believed in portents, unexpected happenings in the natural world that were thought to have prophetic meaning. A portent could be anything from the appearance of a comet to the birth of a deformed animal. The event was usually a sign that some great Roman was soon to die or that the empire was going to suffer some disaster.

were worshiped together in a temple on the Capitoline Hill of Rome from the time of the Etruscan kings; temples to this triad were later built all over the empire.

Mars was originally a god of agriculture; the month of March, when seeds were sown, was named after him. In ancient Rome the new year began in March, so Mars was also the spirit of the year. He later became best known as a god of war—military campaigns began in March, too—perhaps because he was the protector of crops and the land. In March his priests performed dances in which they leaped to encourage the growth of crops and banged spears on shields to drive away evil spirits.

The first temple dedicated to Ceres (SIH-reez), the goddess of agriculture, was built early in the republic in the hope of ending a famine (a severe shortage of food). Plebeians and country people especially worshiped Ceres. Associated with her were the god Liber (LEE-ber) and the goddess Libera (LEE-beh-ruh), who were connected with fertility.

Saturn started out as a numen of sowing and became a god of crops and prosperity. It was said that he had ruled Italy during the long-ago Golden Age. In December the great festival of the Saturnalia was held in his honor, and at this time the Romans tried to re-create the Golden Age as far as possible. During the Saturnalia people gave gifts to one another, slaves dined with their masters, executions were not held, and war could not be declared.

Diana, originally an Italian tree spirit, was a goddess of wild nature, hunting, and the moon. She was a protector of women and children.

Mercury was the god of merchants and travelers. He was also the messenger of the gods. In myths, he and Jupiter often visited Earth together, disguised as common people, in order to check up on mortal behavior.

Two other important Roman gods were Vulcan (VUHL-kuhn), the divine blacksmith, and Neptune, the god of the sea.

Some Greek deities were directly taken over by the Romans. The most important of these was Apollo, god of healing, the sun, music, and poetry. Others were Hercules, who brought success in practical matters; Pluto, the god of the underworld; Aesculapius (ehs-ku-LAY-pee-uhs), another god of healing; and Castor and Pollux, twin gods who protected ships at sea and were famous as horse tamers.

There were also many minor Roman deities, primarily associated with agriculture; most of these were originally numina. Among them were Flora, goddess of flowers; Pomona (puh-MOH-nuh) and her husband, Vertumnus (ver-TUM-nuhs), the goddess and god of fruit and orchards; Carmenta, whose priestesses told the fortunes of children when they were born; Silvanus (sihl-VAH-nuhs), a woodland god who also protected fields and herds; and Faunus (FAW-nuhs), a god of the countryside. Finally, the Romans had many divine personifications, such as Roma, the goddess Rome; Tellus Mater (TEH-lus MAH-ter), "Mother Earth"; Father Tiber, the god of the Tiber River; and Victory.

All of these goddesses and gods were the deities of Rome's official religion. The Romans believed that the prosperity of their state depended on the favor of their deities. In order to gain and keep the divine favor, rituals had to be performed with complete correctness, so worship was highly organized and generally very formal. By the end of the republic, many educated Romans no longer believed in the state-recognized deities, but they continued to worship them for patriotic reasons.

Emperor Worship

Worship of the emperor also became an important part of the state religion. This began after the death of Julius Caesar, when he was declared to have become a god. One reason that Augustus could claim so much authority was that he was therefore the son of a god. Augustus did not allow himself to be worshiped in Rome during his lifetime, but he did encourage the worship of his genius. It made practical sense to the Romans to sacrifice and pray to the guardian spirit of their emperor. In other parts of the empire, however— particularly in the east, where there was a long tradition of ruler worship—Augustus himself was regarded as divine.

After he died, Augustus was made a god of the Roman state, setting a pattern that lasted until late in the third century C.E. Like Hercules, who had been a mortal but was made a god because of his services to humanity, good emperors were routinely deified after their deaths. Not all of them took emperor worship seriously; most regarded it as a tool for uniting the peoples of the empire. Vespasian (vehs-PAY-zhuhn), the ninth emperor, even joked on his deathbed, "Oh dear, I'm afraid I'm becoming a god." A few notorious emperors, however, did insist on being worshiped as gods during their lifetimes.

Fortune and Fate

Although the Roman state used religion to try to keep society stable, many people felt powerless to control their destinies. Life was uncertain and hazardous, full of unpredictable ups and downs caused by some force beyond human understanding. This force was luck or chance, usually personified as the goddess Fortune. Belief in Fortune was strong all over the Roman world (and lasted well into the Middle Ages). Sometimes she was thought of as a guardian of the destinies of communities and individuals. However, people were divided over whether she granted her favors fairly—today to one, tomorrow to another—or whether she was completely fickle and inconsistent. She was blamed when things went wrong at least as much as she was praised when things were going well.

Beginning in the first century B.C.E., people began to blame Fate even more than Fortune. Fate was the unalterable force that planned the whole course of an individual's existence, from birth to death. Belief in Fate usually went along with a strong belief in astrology, which was almost universal in the ancient Mediterranean.

Many felt that it was better to be at the mercy of ordered Fate than of blind Fortune. Others felt that they were somehow controlled by both forces. Cicero was one of the few Romans who seem to have been able to approach these ideas rationally. He wrote that Fate was a series of causes joined together to produce a result, while the idea of Fortune was used when people did not know the causes of present conditions. But to most people of the Roman world, Fate was an inescapable tyrant.

Personal Saviors

The uncertainty of Fortune and the inescapability of Fate weighed heavily on the minds of Romans. In addition there was a great deal of anxiety about what happened to the soul after death. Many people found that the state religion, designed to serve the nation and not the individual, did not fulfill their personal spiritual needs. They felt a longing for a savior who would help them weather the storms of life and guarantee them happiness after death. Large

A mystery ritual dedicated to the Egyptian goddess Isis. The worshipers are being shown sacred symbols related to the goddess's myth. The ritual is led by priests with shaved heads and a priestess draped in red.

numbers of Roman citizens and subjects found such saviors in the mystery religions that flourished particularly during the first centuries of the Common Era.

A mystery religion was one that people joined by going through special ceremonies called initiations. Only worshipers who had been properly prepared could participate in the religion's secret rituals. These usually revolved around a myth of death and rebirth and often included the viewing of sacred objects and the sharing of food and drink. Many mystery rituals were held at night and were powerfully dramatic and emotional. The goal of the rites was to purify believers so that they could commune with the religion's deity or deities and thus rise above worldly cares and the fear of death.

Right: *A fresco from the villa of the Mysteries in Pompeii, where an entire room was painted with scenes showing the worship of Bacchus. Here a child, about to be initiated, reads from a scroll as preparations for a ritual are made.*

The oldest mystery religion practiced in Rome was that of Ceres. This religion had been brought from Greece and was presided over by Greek priestesses. Part of the ceremonies involved acting out the myth of Ceres, whose daughter Proserpina (pruh-SER-pih-nuh) was carried to the underworld by Pluto. Proserpina reigned there as queen of the dead throughout the winter, but returned to Earth and her mother in the spring. It was Ceres's rejoicing at her daughter's return that made the plants, especially the grain, start to grow again.

In Italy only women could participate in these rituals of Ceres. But many Roman men traveled to Greece to participate in the religion's original version, the Eleusinian (ehl-yu-SIH-nee-uhn) mysteries of Demeter (duh-MEE-ter) and Persephone (per-SEH-

fuh-nee). Cicero was one of those who took part in these ceremonies. He wrote afterward, "Nothing is better than those mysteries,
by means of which we are civilized and tamed from a rough and
savage life to a state of humanity. . . . We have received from them
not only a way of living with joy, but even a way of dying with better hope."

Closely related to the mysteries of Ceres were those of
Bacchus (BAH-kuhs), which also came from Greece. Bacchus,
sometimes identified with the old Italian deity Liber, was the god

of wine and inspiration. He was called the liberator of humankind. During his ceremonies the participant was said to become a Bacchus himself or herself. In mythology Bacchus had many female followers, and so women played important roles in this religion. Children could be initiated, too. This was a great comfort to parents if a child died, as often happened in the ancient world, for the mysteries of Bacchus promised that the soul was indestructible and immortal. Just as Bacchus had given eternal life to the human princess Ariadne (a-ree-AD-nee), his beloved wife, so he would give the same gift to his worshipers.

Another Roman mystery god was Mithras (MIHTH-ruhs), originally worshiped in Persia. Mithras was a god of truth and light. In myth he slew a great wild bull that was the first living creature. From the bull's blood sprang grain and other good gifts. Then the first human couple was born, and Mithras had to defend them from the powers of evil. When his work on Earth was completed, he feasted with the sun god. His worshipers imitated the feast in their rituals, which took place in underground chapels. Only men were accepted into this religion, and they had to go through many physical ordeals to become initiates. Mithraism especially appealed to soldiers, who spread it throughout the empire.

The Great Goddesses

The most frenzied of all the mystery religions was that of Cybele (KIH-buh-lee), the Great Mother of Anatolia (Asia Minor). The first image of Cybele was brought to Rome in 204 B.C.E., and the goddess joined the deities of the state religion. Beginning in the first century C.E., her worship became increasingly popular, and the rituals of her homeland came to be celebrated not only in Rome but all over the empire. Every year a major festival in honor of Cybele and her young lover Attis began on March 15. In addition to the secret ceremonies were public ones, including processions in which a statue of the goddess was carried through the streets while coins and rose petals were strewn along the route and armed men danced to the music of tambourines, cymbals, flutes, and horns. For the first seven days of the festival the worshipers fasted. Then, on March 22, a freshly cut pine tree was decorated

Mithras slaying the bull

with ribbons and purple flowers and carried into Cybele's sanctuary. This tree was a symbol of Attis, who according to myth died under a pine tree. For two days the worshipers mourned for the dead Attis. Next, on March 24, came the Day of Blood, when many participants lashed and cut themselves in order to identify with Attis's suffering. March 25 was a day of feasting and rejoicing to celebrate Attis's return to life, followed by a day of rest. On the final day of the festival, March 27, Cybele's image was ritually washed in a river before being returned to the temple.

Although Cybele was called the Great Mother, the most popular deity in the Roman world during the time of the emperors was the Egyptian goddess Isis. There were rituals in honor of Isis every day, and splendid festivals several times a year. The most joyful of these was the Finding of Osiris (oh-SY-rihs), in mid-November. Osiris was Isis's husband. His jealous brother Set had sealed him inside a wooden chest and put it into the Nile River. The chest floated out to sea, and Isis sorrowfully searched for it until she at last found it in Lebanon. To her grief, Set then cut Osiris's body into fourteen pieces and scattered them throughout Egypt. Isis painstakingly gathered them together and with her magic restored Osiris, who became king of the underworld. Their son, Horus (HO-ruhs), took vengeance on Set for his parents' suffering.

Isis was all things to all people. She was a devoted wife and a loving mother, a just ruler, and a powerful magician. She was a goddess of love, of the moon, and of the sea. She was called the Queen of Heaven, the Queen of War, the Lawgiver, and the Glory of Women. She was said to have invented languages and alphabets and to have divided the Earth from heaven.

People from every level of society were welcomed into the religion of Isis. Women flocked to her worship, and she gave them equality with men. Initiates of Isis were strengthened in life by the goddess's awesome power to overcome Fate and Fortune. When they died, Isis assured them of resurrection (a life after death).

The Beginning of a New Order

At the same time that Isis enjoyed her greatest popularity, another religion that promised resurrection was steadily growing. This was

JEWS IN THE ROMAN EMPIRE

There were large Jewish communities throughout the eastern part of the empire as well as in what is now Israel. Unfortunately the Jews were generally disliked, distrusted, and misunderstood (although individual Jews often rose to prominent positions). Jewish culture was entirely different from Greco-Roman culture. The Jews believed in the existence of only one god, and their lives were governed by their religious laws and customs. They lived in tightly knit communities of their own and seemed to want to have nothing to do with the non-Jews around them.

Rome's usual tact in dealing with conquered peoples broke down tragically when it came to the Jews. Beginning with Pompey's entrance into the most sacred part of the Jerusalem temple in 63 B.C.E., Romans repeatedly insulted Jewish religious feelings. Nevertheless, for a time Judaea enjoyed a large degree of self-government under Roman rule, and the Jewish religion was officially tolerated. The situation worsened after the death of Augustus, and at last, in 66 C.E., Judaea rose in rebellion. The revolt was ruthlessly crushed by the emperor Vespasian and his son, the future emperor Titus, who destroyed Jerusalem and its temple. There were two more Jewish revolts in the second century, and these also failed completely. The Jewish nation was annihilated, to be reborn only in the twentieth century.

Christianity. Like the mystery religions, Christianity offered people a personal savior. Christian groups, which were open to people from all walks of life, were closely knit and very firm in their beliefs. Unfortunately the new religion was widely misunderstood. Moreover, Christians refused to participate in the state religion— an extremely unpatriotic and even treasonable act in Roman eyes. For these reasons Christians were sometimes blamed for the empire's problems and persecuted in times of national crisis. But in 313 C.E. the emperor Constantine I issued the Edict of Mediolanum (modern Milan), which proclaimed tolerance for Christianity. Constantine himself became a Christian, and Christianity became the official religion of the Roman Empire for the rest of the empire's existence.

CHAPTER FOUR

THE ROMAN WAY OF LIFE

The Roman state endures because of its ancient morals and its manhood.

—Ennius (Roman poet)

A father holding his child. This scene is part of a relief on a child's sarcophagus (stone coffin).

Patriotism and the Roman Virtues

The guiding principle of ancient Rome was patriotism. As we have seen, the arts and even religion were made to serve the state. A career in public service was the highest calling. Romans were expected to always act "for the good of the commonwealth," even if their own interests suffered. The rights and responsibilities of citizenship were taken very seriously, and a citizen's personal behavior was seen as having a direct effect on the well-being of the state.

The ancient Romans were convinced that they were the most virtuous as well as the most powerful people in the world—in fact, it was because of their superior virtues that they had been destined to rule over all other nations. They believed that no other people excelled as they did in courage, dignity, discipline, good faith, piety, and mercy. They expected themselves to live up to these serious and practical values without fail. But during the second half of Rome's long existence, there were many who felt that the state and people had become corrupt. These reformers constantly urged the Romans to return to the traditions of their ancestors.

Patrons and Clients

One of Rome's most ancient and important institutions was *clientela* (klee-uhn-TEH-luh). This was a special hereditary relationship between a wealthy patrician patron and a poor (but free) plebeian client. The patron gave his clients financial and legal help, and

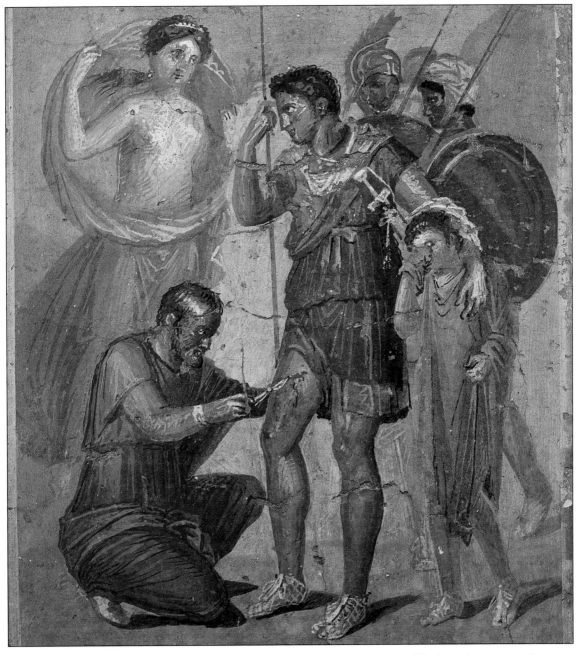

The hero Aeneas was the embodiment of the Roman virtues. Here, with his son at his side, he stands unflinching as a wound in his leg is probed by a doctor. The goddess Venus, Aeneas's mother, looks on.

clients gave their patron political help. This meant that in elections a client always voted for his patron or his patron's relatives or friends, and a client who served in the Assembly supported only legislation that was supported by his patron.

Although *clientela* was a very practical system, a great deal of emotion was attached to it. A patron was supposed to regard his clients more highly than he regarded his relatives by marriage, while a client owed his patron the same respect as he owed his parents, the nation, and the deities. *Clientela* was always to be governed by good faith, personified as the goddess Fides (FEE-days).

The relationship between patron and client had such powerful emotional and religious associations for the Romans that they carried it over into other areas of activity. When Rome expanded, some of the new territories became "client states," with Rome as their patron. Military commanders set themselves up as the patrons of their soldiers. *Clientela* was carried to its greatest extreme when Augustus (and then the emperors who followed him) proclaimed that all Roman citizens were his clients.

A SENATOR'S DAY

A Roman senator was awake well before dawn, working on his accounts, dictating letters to his secretary, and taking care of other business in the *tablinum* of his home. When he was done he went into the atrium, where his clients came to ask his help and advice or simply to pay their respects. Some mornings the senator might have a wedding or other special event to attend instead of greeting his clients.

After these early-morning activities, the senator went to the Forum, accompanied by his clients. (If it was a holiday, though, he might go to the circus, the amphitheater, or the theater.) The law courts and the Senate met from nine to eleven. Then there was a break for lunch, followed by an hour or more of rest. If necessary, courts and Senate reconvened and continued until three or four o'clock.

Usually, however, the afternoon was devoted to recreation. First a senator might go to the Campus Martius (KAM-puhs MAR-shuhs) to exercise. The Campus was the old drill ground for the Roman army, and here men practiced riding, fencing, archery, wrestling, boxing, and other soldierly skills. There were also ball games and what we would call track-and-field sports. Men of all ages and all walks of life exercised on the Campus. After exercise some men might take a swim in the Tiber. Others would go to the public baths.

Around four in the afternoon it was dinnertime. A senator was nearly always either hosting or attending dinner parties. These dinners consisted of at least three courses and could be very elaborate. The diners reclined on couches around the table; they brought with them their own napkins. At smaller dinner parties the main entertainment was conversation, but at grand banquets performers would dance, juggle, play music, and so on. Dinner usually lasted for three or four hours and might be followed by a late-night drinking party. Usually, however, senators were home and in bed quite early, preparing for another busy day.

The Family

The family was the foundation of Roman society. A traditional Roman family consisted of the head of the household, called the *pater familias* (PAH-ter fah-MEEL-yuhs); his wife; his unmarried daughters; his sons; and his sons' wives, unmarried daughters, and sons.

The Power of the Father

The *pater familias* was the absolute authority in the family. He controlled all the property and made all the decisions. Only he was legally independent—the other family members were, according to the letter of the law, his personal property. He arranged his children's and grandchildren's marriages and could also order these marriages to be ended in divorce. He had to consent to his sons' and grandsons' career choices. He had the power to decide whether newborn children would be raised in the household or be disowned. If a family member strayed outside the bounds of proper behavior, the *pater familias* could punish the offender with sentences as severe as banishment, slavery, or death. Augustus, for example, banished both his daughter and his granddaughter for immoral conduct.

This *patria potestas* (PAH-tree-uh poh-TEHS-tuhs), "power of the father," was limited to some extent by custom and public opinion: The reputation of a *pater familias* was severely damaged if he inflicted needlessly cruel punishments or wasted the family property. A man holding public office was freed from *patria potestas* for as long as his term lasted. Men who became priests of Jupiter and women who became Vestal Virgins were permanently released from *patria potestas*. And sometimes a father would emancipate, or free, a child, who then was legally a family in his or her own right. When a *pater familias* died, each of his sons became the *pater familias* of his own household.

Roman Women

In some forms of marriage, a woman did not come under the control of her husband, but remained part of her father's family. In any case, all women officially had guardians (husbands, fathers, or other males) to handle their legal and financial affairs. However, women could inherit property and were frequently able to control it themselves thanks to loopholes in the law. And when husbands were away at war, as they so often were, or holding government posts in the provinces, wives commonly took charge of all the family business.

Except for Vestal Virgins, all Roman women were expected to marry and have children. The ideal Roman matron (upper-class married woman) married only once, but in reality divorce and remarriage were common. (In a divorce the father always got custody of the children.) Similarly, although women who bore many children were singled out for special praise (and Augustus's laws gave them special privileges), most upper-class women had only one to three children.

Roman matrons were expected to spin and weave, to direct the running of the household, and to oversee their children's educations. However, they were also free to visit friends, shop, attend public shows, relax at the baths, take part in festivals and religious rituals (many for women only), and accompany their husbands to dinner parties. In addition, although they could not vote or hold public office, Roman matrons exercised a great deal of behind-the-scenes political power. On a few occasions large groups of women even held political demonstrations in the Forum, and from time to time a woman orator spoke in the law courts or Senate. Some upper-class women owned their own businesses or actively participated in running family businesses.

This Roman husband and wife were clearly proud of their ability to read and write—he holds a scroll (the Roman form of book), and she holds a wax-covered tablet and a stylus for writing on it.

Lower-class women worked at a number of occupations. There were spinners, weavers, shopkeepers, butchers, fishers, midwives, millers, waitresses, entertainers, and prostitutes. Less common—but still present—were secretaries, physicians, landladies, moneylenders, businesswomen, and construction workers.

Roman women enjoyed much more freedom than women in

many other parts of the ancient world, notably Greece. Nevertheless Roman society was strongly geared toward men. There were separate standards of conduct for men and women. For example adultery was perfectly acceptable for men but was illegal for women. Roman matrons were expected to be highly virtuous at all times. When women behaved immorally, their conduct was thought to seriously endanger the well-being of the state.

Children

Sons were definitely preferred to daughters: One of the oldest Roman laws ruled that fathers must rear all of their sons but had to raise only the firstborn daughter. Girls did not even have names of their own, but bore the feminine forms of their fathers' first names. All daughters in a family therefore had the same name, with "the elder," "the younger," or a number added to tell them apart. Still, the daughters who were raised seem to have been cared for and loved just as much as the sons.

Immediately after birth a baby was laid at the father's feet. If he took it in his arms, it was acknowledged as his own and was admitted into full membership in the family. Otherwise the child was taken out and left by the roadside to die or be picked up by slave traders. However, this seems to have happened only rarely.

Eight or nine days after birth, there was a solemn ritual in

The remains of a Roman child's well-loved rag doll

Roman children playing ball

which the baby was purified and given its name. On this day the father placed around the child's neck a special locket called a *bulla,* which contained an amulet for protection against evil. The child also received small metal charms from family friends, relatives, and household slaves. These were strung on a necklace both to protect the baby and to entertain it with their jingling.

As children grew older they had many kinds of toys. Among them were rag dolls and dolls of clay and wax, ivory letters, hobby-horses, tops, stilts, balls, and miniature carts and wagons (sometimes pulled by mice, according to the poet Horace). There were also board games and games like hide-and-seek, jacks, marbles, and others. Many children had pet dogs, cats, or birds.

Education began at home. Parents instructed their children—from a very early age—in the Roman virtues of truthfulness, self-reliance, piety, respect for law, and obedience to authority. Even in homes where much of the child care was provided by slaves,

A teacher and two students. The teacher is probably a Greek slave or freedman, as most teachers were.

children spent a great deal of time with their parents. In this way they learned much about the roles they would be expected to fill as adults.

Relatively few Roman children went to school. Most of those who did were boys from noble or wealthy families. Poor children usually had to work, and girls generally continued to be educated at home. In school, studies centered on the art of public speaking. During the republic, mastery of this art was essential for upper-class men, who were expected to play an active role in politics. The arts and sciences were studied hardly at all.

A boy's schooling continued until he officially became an adult, around the age of sixteen. There was a great ceremony to celebrate a boy's coming-of-age, usually held on March 17, a festival called the Liberalia. Early in the morning, the boy laid his *bulla* and childhood garment before the Lares. After a sacrifice was performed, the *bulla* was hung up, to be worn again only if the boy later achieved great fame and needed the amulet to protect him from envy. The boy then dressed in a white tunic, which had crimson stripes if his father was a member of the Senate or *equites*. Over this tunic his father draped the toga virilis, the garment of a man. Next the boy was escorted to the Forum by his father and his father's friends, relatives, clients, slaves, and freedmen. In the Forum the boy proudly added his name to the list of citizens. After the family

A bride (standing, center) *prepares for her wedding with the help of her mother.*

made an offering at the temple of the god Liber, they returned home for a dinner party in honor of the new citizen.

For all intents and purposes, a girl's coming-of-age ceremony was her wedding. The night before the ceremony, she gave the Lares her *bulla* and often her childhood toys (girls married as young as twelve). The next morning, before sunrise, her mother dressed her for the wedding, which was held at home. There were several different types of wedding ceremony, but in all of them the essential feature was the bride's expression of consent to the marriage. After the ceremony, there was a dinner that lasted until evening. Then the groom took the bride from her mother's arms, and a merry procession escorted her to her new husband's home. Upon arrival she wound bands of wool around the doorposts and anointed the door with oil and fat as symbols of prosperity and happiness. Then the groom carried her over the threshold. In the atrium he offered her fire and water, and she lit a new fire in the hearth. At last the couple was led to their wedding couch and left alone to begin married life.

Slavery

The Romans did not believe in social or political equality. The relationships between people of different classes were regulated by both law and custom. All male citizens could vote, but poor clients had to vote as their rich patrons wished. For the most part public office was held only by wealthy, upper-class men who came from families that had a long tradition of serving in the Senate. And although wealthy and middle-class Romans enjoyed one of the highest standards of living in the ancient world, this was made possible largely because of slavery.

The existence of slavery was taken for granted in most ancient societies, but the Romans made greater use of slaves than any culture before theirs had done. From the third century B.C.E. onward, slavery became extremely widespread and important to the Roman economy. Wealthy Romans had hundreds or even thousands of slaves working their lands and serving them in their homes. It is estimated that in the time of Augustus, at least one-quarter of the one million people living in the city of Rome were

IF YOU LIVED IN ANCIENT ROME

If you had been born in ancient Rome, your way of life would have been determined by the facts of your birth—whether you were a girl or a boy, slave or free, wealthy or poor. With this chart you can trace the course your life might have taken as a member of the Roman upper class.

You were born into the Roman nobility. . . .

As a Boy . . .   As a Girl . . .

You live in a one- or two-story house in town and often spend time at your family's country home as well. You play with toys and may have pets. Slaves help care for you, but you spend a great deal of time with your parents, too. Your mother teaches you to read, write, and do simple arithmetic.

At age 7 you attend school, where you learn the art of public speaking, grammar, literature, law, Greek, and other subjects. You are taught to swim, ride, wrestle, box, hunt, and use weapons. When you are not in school, you are with your father, observing the proper conduct of a Roman gentleman.

▼

Around age 16 you officially become an adult. You spend a year as an apprentice to a lawyer, government official, or other notable man. You may go to Greece or Asia Minor to study philosophy and other advanced subjects. At age 17 you can be called up for military service. You probably marry soon.

▼

Your adult life is busy and productive, but there is also plenty of leisure time. You may be away from Rome a great deal, with the army or in the provinces. When you are home you take an active part in your sons' upbringing. At age 30 you are eligible to run for public office. When your father dies, you become an independent *pater familias*.

At age 7 you are your mother's constant companion. She teaches you to spin, weave, sew, and manage a household. You might have a tutor or attend elementary school for a time. You may also learn to sing and play the lyre.

▼

Between the ages of 12 and 15 you are married, probably to a man chosen by your father, but with your consent. Your family gives you clothing, jewelry, and slaves to take with you to your new home.

▼

As a Roman matron you are highly respected. In addition to running your household and caring for your children, you spend much time in social activities. You assist your husband in his career and help him manage the family property. If you are divorced or widowed, you may remarry or remain single.

In your old age you receive great respect, according to Roman tradition. When you die your body is buried or cremated, with the remains placed in a family tomb outside the city walls. A son or other male relative may deliver a eulogy for you in the Forum.

slaves. On the Italian peninsula as a whole, slaves may have made up as much as one-third of the total population.

In early times, people could be enslaved for not paying their debts. Later most Roman slaves were prisoners of war or their descendants. Other slaves were people captured and sold by Mediterranean pirates. Very poor people often abandoned or sold their children, who ended up as slaves. Wherever they came from, slaves were legally not people but property.

Many slaves were treated cruelly. They were branded to show who owned them. They worked at hard labor from sunup to sundown. They were flogged for disobedience. When they were too old or ill to work, their food rations were reduced. They were sent to the arena to fight and die as gladiators or as victims of wild animals. Slave families were broken up and sold to different owners. If a slave murdered the master, all of the master's slaves, including children, were put to death.

Given the inhuman treatment experienced by large numbers of slaves, it is not surprising that from time to time there were slave rebellions. During the second century B.C.E., these uprisings occurred especially often. There were two very large rebellions in Sicily, in which slaves overran the island. In 73–71 B.C.E. the gladiator Spartacus led an army of ninety thousand slaves in a revolt in southern Italy. His goal was to have foreign slaves be allowed to return to their homelands. None of the slave rebellions were successful, and more than a million slaves lost their lives in them.

Kindness and Freedom

Not all slaves had a desire to rebel. In fact many Roman slaves were much better off than the free poor. The slaves always had food to eat and a place to live. It was not uncommon for slaves and masters to become close friends. Both male and female slaves who served in wealthy homes often received education and special training. Men might work as secretaries, readers, doctors, teachers, or artists. Women were trained as secretaries, readers, hairdressers, ladies' maids, midwives, nurses, entertainers, or masseuses. Slaves could run their own businesses, although of course their owners received most of the profits; a majority of the small traders in Rome were in fact slaves. In the household of the emperor, slaves

A slave girl stands ready to serve her mistress, who is playing a stringed instrument.

held important positions as administrators and civil servants.

A unique feature of Roman slavery was that slaves were allowed to save up money of their own, which they could use to buy their freedom. (They could also use this money, as they often did, to buy their own slaves.) In addition slave owners frequently freed their slaves as a reward for good service or granted them freedom in their wills. Childless couples sometimes freed and then adopted their favorite slaves.

Freed slaves became clients of their former owners and continued to owe them service. If the owner was a Roman citizen, the freed slave became a citizen, too. Freedmen and freedwomen carried on a number of trades, especially if they had received special training while slaves. Freedmen frequently held administrative and religious posts. It was not uncommon for freed slaves to become quite wealthy and live in great luxury. The sons and descendants of freed slaves were allowed to hold public office and might even rise to the top of the Roman social order.

A Lasting Source of Civilization

In 609 C.E. the Pantheon was consecrated as a Christian church. This painting by Giovanni Paolo Pannini shows the interior of the Pantheon as it looked around 1750. The columns, floor, and dome are as they were in Roman times. It looks very much the same today.

In regions that were part of the empire, numerous remains of Roman buildings are still standing. Some are even still in use. Several amphitheaters and theaters have been restored, and operas, concerts, and plays are now presented in them. There are Roman roads, bridges, and aqueducts that continued to serve people until well into the twentieth century. And works of art produced under the Romans can be seen in museums all over the world. But as magnificent as these things are, they form only a small part of Rome's legacy.

The Fate of the Empire

In 364 C.E., the Roman Empire was divided into western and eastern halves. The Greek-speaking eastern empire, with its capital at Constantinople, developed into the splendid Byzantine Empire, which lasted until 1453. The western empire, however, was overrun by Germanic invaders and swiftly crumbled. In 476 the last Roman emperor, Romulus Augustulus (aw-GUS-tyoo-luhs), was overthrown by the barbarian general Odoacer (OH-duh-way-ser), who declared himself king of Italy. The Roman state's one-thousand-year existence had come to an end.

After the fall of the western empire, its former territories began to develop into individual nations. Yet these separate states were still culturally united in many ways because of their common Roman heritage.

THE HOLY ROMAN EMPIRE

Long after its fall, the idea of the Roman Empire remained strong in Europe, and attempts were made to recapture its power. In 800 C.E. Charlemagne (SHAR-luh-mane), ruler of lands stretching from France to central Europe, was widely felt to have revived the western Roman Empire. He was therefore crowned emperor by the pope in Rome. Charlemagne's court was a scene of great artistic and intellectual activity, and much importance was given to the study of classical Latin and the literature of ancient Rome. Unfortunately, despite its magnificence, Charlemagne's empire fell apart under his grandsons.

In 962 the German king Otto I followed in Charlemagne's footsteps and was likewise crowned emperor by the pope. The German and Italian territories that he and his successors ruled became known as the Holy Roman Empire. The original concept behind this empire was that the Christian world should have a single political authority, in harmony with the religious authority of the pope. However, there were power struggles between emperor and pope throughout the empire's existence. The Holy Roman Empire had a long history—it lasted until 1806—but it never attained the political or cultural force of ancient Rome.

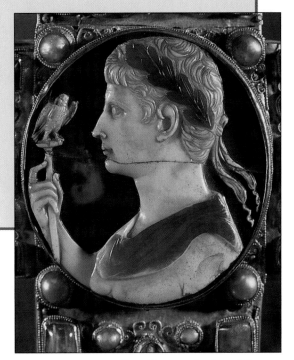

Otto II, second ruler of the Holy Roman Empire, had this cameo (gem carving) of Augustus made to decorate the center of a jeweled cross. The cameo is clearly inspired by similar carved gems from ancient Rome.

Religion

In all of these regions Roman Catholic Christianity was the established religion. (In the seventh century, however, North Africa and much of Spain would be converted to Islam.) As the church had grown, especially after its legal approval by Constantine, it had developed a structure very similar to the structure of the empire's government. The head of the church was the bishop of Rome, the pope. Under his authority were all the other bishops, who were geographically spread out, rather like provincial governors. They in turn had charge of all the individual Christian communities in their areas. There were still many disagreements over specific beliefs and practices, but the early church was nevertheless able both to survive and to expand, largely thanks to its Roman-type organization. It might even be said that the church, ruled from Rome, became a new kind of religious empire.

63

Pope John Paul II investing new cardinals in 1994. The pope is the head of the Roman Catholic Church, which in many ways is still run on the model of the government of the Roman Empire.

Ancient Roman religion left many legacies to Roman Catholicism, including the use of candles, incense, altars, statues, set rituals, special priestly garments, and choral singing. Quite a few churches were built on the sites of Roman temples, and in some cases (most notably the Pantheon) temples were converted into churches. Similarly the dates of many Christian holidays were set to replace Roman and other pre-Christian festivals. The pope's formal title, Pontifex Maximus (PAHN-tih-fex MAX-ih-muhs), is the same as the title of the chief priest of ancient Rome (an office once held by Julius Caesar).

Other aspects of Roman culture also lived on in Christianity. Early church buildings—and many later ones, too—were modeled on a type of Roman building called a basilica, a rectangular roofed hall that served as a meeting place and law court. And until the 1960s, all Roman Catholic rituals were conducted in Latin.

Language

Christian missionaries carried their religion all over Europe, and along with it went the Latin language. As a result, Latin spread even to areas that had never been under Roman rule. For more than a thousand years after the fall of Rome, Latin was understood by nearly every educated person in Europe. It was the language of scholarship and often of government and literature, as well as of religion.

In most of the European countries that had once been part of the Roman world, Latin also continued to be the language spoken by the common people. This spoken Latin slowly changed, evolving into what are called the Romance languages. The major Romance languages—used by millions of people today—are Italian, French, Spanish, Portuguese, and Romanian.

The Latin language has also made a huge contribution to English. Most of the prefixes in English come from Latin, and so do many entire words, sometimes little changed from their ancient forms. In addition many fields, such as medicine and especially law, have specialized vocabularies that use a great many Latin terms.

Law

From the time of the Twelve Tables until the last century of the empire, the Romans were constantly formulating laws and legal

---

SPEAKING LATIN

Many words that we use every day come from Latin, including the names of the months and most of the planets. Here are some others.

Politics and Government
candidate
committee
congress
conservative
constitution
election
governor
legislature
liberal
majority
minority
republican
senate

The Arts
actor
audience
author
camera
director
editor
literature

mural
novel
opera
statue
verse
video

Science
evolution
friction
gravity
liquid
particle
radiation
solid
species
vacuum

Education
campus
college
course
history
language
library

pupil
student
university

Measurement
acre
century
decade
decimal
meter
mile
ounce
quart
volume

Military
admiral
army
commander
company
corporal
defense
general
navy

Food
asparagus
cereal
fruit
herb
onion
pork
radish

Law
court
judge
jury
legal
verdict

Architecture
arch
cement
concrete
exterior
interior

theories. Cicero wrote that a state without law was like a body without a mind, and pointed out that law was the ultimate safeguard of the rights and privileges of citizens. The outstanding characteristic of Roman law was practical common sense.

Jurists, men who were especially learned in the law, sat in on trials, advised officials and judges, assisted citizens in legal matters, and answered questions of law that were presented to them. They made their rulings based on custom, experience, comparison with previous rulings, and general standards of reasonableness and fairness. The principles worked out by the Roman jurists formed the basis of the legal systems and law codes of many of the developing European nations. In these countries and others that they have influenced (for example, the former Spanish colonies of Latin America), Roman law is still functioning to some extent today. The Roman jurists' concept of law as written reason was also a most valuable contribution to future legal thought.

Roman law was originally concerned only with relationships between citizens. As Rome expanded, however, it was necessary to formulate legal principles for dealing with noncitizens and foreigners. And so the Roman jurists created the "law of nations," one of the most powerful ideas in the history of the world. According to the law of nations, there were certain legal principles that applied equally to everyone regardless of whether or not they were Roman citizens. The law of nations gradually evolved into the philosophical notion of "natural law," a set of principles based in nature and felt to be valid anywhere in the world at any time. Later the law of nations expanded to cover the rules governing relationships between states. This was the beginning of international law, a major force for peace and order in the world community, most prominently embodied today by the United Nations.

Rebirth: The Renaissance

In the centuries after the fall of Rome, the church came to be the central force in European culture. Most architecture, art, and literature were produced in its service. Education, too, was largely religious in nature, intended mainly to prepare men for the priesthood.

In Italy in the fourteenth and fifteenth centuries, all that began to change. Urban life was again flourishing, and city-states had become the major political units. Italian intellectuals had a fresh spirit of patriotism and a strong sense that they were living at the beginning of a new age, one that would re-create the splendor of classical (meaning Greco-Roman) civilization. Scholars, statesmen, architects, artists, and writers all turned to ancient Rome—and, to a somewhat lesser extent, Greece—for inspiration. This movement was called the Renaissance, meaning "rebirth"—the rebirth of classical culture. From Italy the Renaissance spread all over Europe.

Renaissance artists and writers copied classical forms and styles, and produced works that were based on Greek and Roman mythology and literature. Architects designed buildings that used elements of classical architecture; the dome of the Pantheon in particular was often imitated. Roman history and Greek philosophy gave people in many fields valuable social, political, and ethical lessons and models.

The most far-reaching aspect of the Renaissance was humanism. This began as a movement to reform education and make it more open and useful to a wide range of students, not just those who were going to become priests. Humanists recommended a course of study using classical texts and based on traditional Roman education, with the main subjects being literature, grammar, public speaking, history, and ethics. Together these subjects were called the humanities.

Like the Romans, humanists believed that an education in the humanities involved students' characters as well as their minds and

The Tempietto nel Chiostro, in the courtyard of a monastery in Rome, was built in 1499. The architect, Bramante, was inspired by a Roman temple dedicated to the sibyl (a mythical woman prophet).

67

Artists from the Renaissance on turned to Ovid's Metamorphoses *to find subjects for their work. This painting by German artist Lucas Cranach (1475–1553) illustrates Ovid's story of Pyramus and Thisbe, tragic young lovers. Thinking that Thisbe had been eaten by a lion, Pyramus killed himself. When Thisbe found his body, she, too, committed suicide.*

The seventeenth-century Italian architect and sculptor Bernini got the idea for this dramatic statue of Apollo and Daphne from a story in Ovid's Metamorphoses. *Apollo loved the beautiful Daphne, but she did not return the god's love. When he pursued her, she fled, praying for help. Just as Apollo caught up to her, she was turned into a laurel tree.*

gave them the best preparation for the responsibilities of citizenship and full participation in society. This ideal has had a profound impact on education ever since. It is the foundation of modern liberal arts education, which seeks to expose students to a wide range of general knowledge and to develop their ability to reason and think for themselves.

Humanism soon became much more than an educational movement. The humanists saw that classical literature focused on concrete human concerns and the realities of this world. They were especially influenced by the works of Cicero, who wrote frequently on the subject of *humanitas* (hoo-MAH-nee-tas), "humanity," as both an educational and a social ideal. All people, said Cicero, share in the divine and are related as brothers. Therefore even the humblest person deserves respect, and human beings should always help one another—in this way they are living according to

THE PRESERVATION OF GREEK CULTURE

When the Romans commissioned copies of Greek works of art, patronized the use of Greek architectural and artistic forms, interpreted Greek philosophy, and translated Greek literature, they were making one of their most significant contributions to the world: the preservation of ancient Greek culture. Although Roman writings were known to scholars of the Middle Ages, Greek writings were known only in Latin versions. Not until the Renaissance did people learn to read ancient Greek again and so gain firsthand knowledge of Greek literature and thought. Even today, our best idea of ancient Greek sculpture comes from Roman copies.

BUILDING A LEGACY

The revival of Roman architectural styles that began in the Renaissance lasted well into the twentieth century. It reached its peak in the eighteenth and early nineteenth centuries, when many buildings in the Roman style were constructed with archaeological exactness. Thomas Jefferson designed several such buildings for the campus of the University of Virginia, as well as the Virginia State capitol, which he modeled on a Roman temple. In the twentieth century a modernized Roman style emerged in the United States and was used for a number of public buildings, including the New York Public Library and Boston's Museum of Fine Arts.

Low Library of Columbia University in New York City is a good example of the modernized Roman style of architecture that was popular in the United States early in the twentieth century.

the divinity in their souls. The humanists shared this outlook, and celebrated human dignity and the worth of the individual. Such humanist ideas are still fundamental to Western civilization.

The Enlightenment

Humanism received new importance in the eighteenth-century literary and philosophical movement known as the Enlightenment. Enlightenment writers carried humanist ideas even further than in the Renaissance, focusing on the goodness and perfectibility of humankind and especially on the power of human reason. Again Rome provided much inspiration. The influence of Roman thought is especially clear in the Enlightenment's emphasis on common sense and natural law.

Among the people most moved by such ideals were the founders of the United States. The majority of them had received humanistic educations and were well-read in classical literature, for which they had a deep love. As always, one of the most influential classical authors was Cicero. His works gained extra relevance because, like his eighteenth-century readers, he had lived through a time of great political upheaval. Thomas Jefferson said that much of his inspiration came from Cicero's political writings, and John Adams spent the summer before he became the second president of the United States reading Cicero's essays.

The founders turned to Greek and Roman history, philosophy, and literature for entertainment, examples of strength in the face of hardship, models of patriotic conduct, moral guidance, military advice, political wisdom, and more. Much of what they learned from the Greeks and Romans inspired the writing of the Declaration of Independence, the Constitution, and the Bill of Rights. Indeed the government of the United States was based largely on the model of the Roman Republic.

The representative democracy of the United States in turn became a model for political developments in other countries, as it continues to be today. In this as in so many other ways, much of the best of Roman culture lives on. Rome may have fallen more than fifteen hundred years ago, but its legacy will continue for generations to come.

The Romans: A Chronology

B.C.E.

753	Legendary founding of Rome by Romulus
509	Beginning of the Roman Republic
c. 496	First temple of Ceres built
c. 494	Creation of the office of tribune
451–449	Formulation and publication of the Twelve Tables
431	First temple of Apollo built in Rome
312	Construction of the Appian Way
300	Plebeians may hold any office in the republic
293	Worship of Aesculapius brought to Rome
290	End of Samnite Wars
272	Rome gains control of entire Italian peninsula
264–241	First Punic War
218–201	Second Punic War
204	First image of goddess Cybele brought to Rome
200–196	Second Macedonian War
171–168	Third Macedonian War
149–146	Third Punic War
146	Annexation of Greece
139–132	First slave revolt in Sicily
133	Tiberius Gracchus is tribune
129	Creation of province of Asia
123–122	Gaius Gracchus is tribune
121	Annexation of Gallia Narbonensis (southern France)
112–105	Jugurthine War in Numidia
104–100	Second slave revolt in Sicily
102–101	Marius defeats Celtic-Germanic Cimbri and Teutones
91–87	Social War
88	First consulship of Sulla
87–84	First Mithradatic War
81	Dictatorship of Sulla; Second Mithradatic War
80	Second consulship of Sulla
73–71	Slave revolt led by Spartacus
70	Consulships of Pompey and Crassus
66–63	Pompey clears the Mediterranean of pirates, defeats Mithradates, conquers Syria, and makes Judaea a Roman client
63	Consulship of Cicero; conspiracy of Catiline
60	Formation of First Triumvirate
59	Consulship of Caesar
58–51	Caesar conquers Gaul
55	First permanent theater in Rome built by Pompey; death of Lucretius

54	Death of Catullus
49–45	Civil War
44	Murder of Caesar
43	Formation of Second Triumvirate; death of Cicero
31	Octavius defeats Antony and Cleopatra
30	Annexation of Egypt
27	Octavius becomes Augustus, rules empire alone
19	Death of Virgil
B.C.E. **16–9** C.E.	Empire's northern boundary extended to Danube River
8	Death of Horace
c. 6	Birth of Jesus

C.E.

14	Death of Augustus
17	Deaths of Ovid and Livy
c. 30	Death of Jesus
43–46	Annexation of Britain
65	Death of Seneca
66	Death of Petronius
69–79	Reign of Vespasian
70	Titus destroys Jerusalem (end of First Jewish Revolt)
79	Eruption of Mount Vesuvius destroys Pompeii and Herculaneum
80	Opening of Flavian Amphitheater (Colosseum)
98–117	Reign of Trajan
106	Annexation of Dacia
109	Eleven aqueducts serve Rome
117–138	Reign of Hadrian
120	Death of Tacitus
127	Death of Juvenal
138–161	Reign of Antoninus Pius
161–180	Reign of Marcus Aurelius
167–172	War against Germanic Marcomanni
after 170	Death of Apuleius
177–180	War against Germanic Sarmatians
306–337	Reign of Constantine I
313	Edict of Mediolanum (Milan) favors Christianity
330	Constantinople becomes capital of Roman Empire
364	Empire is divided into eastern and western halves
476	Overthrow of last emperor of western empire

This chronology gives dates only for events that are mentioned or referred to in this book.

GLOSSARY

amphitheater: an oval building for gladiatorial contests and other spectacles

aqueduct: an artificial channel to carry water from its source to a city

astrology: the interpretation of the positions of the sun, moon, and planets as they are believed to influence human lives

atrium: the front room of a Roman house

augur: a priest who examined the internal organs of animals in order to discover the will of the deities

bulla: a locket, usually of gold, containing a protective amulet, worn by children

circus: a long oval building for chariot races and other shows

clientela: the relationship between a wealthy patrician patron and a poor but free client; patron and client were obligated to help each other in various ways

consul: one of two head magistrates elected every year

deify: to make into a deity

equites: the wealthy class of knights, which became the banking and business class

forum: the civic center and main meeting place of a Roman city, with government buildings, law courts, and temples surrounding a large open area

fresco: a wall painting made while the plaster is still wet

genius: a man's guardian spirit

gladiator: a professional fighter, usually a slave, who fought to the death in public shows

insula: an apartment building

juno: a woman's guardian spirit

Lares: divine guardians of the family

manes: spirits of the dead

matron: an upper-class married woman

mosaic: a picture or design made of tiny colored tiles

numen: the divine force in a specific activity or place

pater familias: the male head of a household

patria potestas: a father's power over all the other family members

patrician: a member of Rome's ancient upper class

personification: a deity or imaginary being that represents a thing or idea

plebeian: a member of the ancient freeborn lower class

portent: an unexpected occurrence in nature, thought to be a sign of future events

relief: a form of sculpture in which the images project out from a flat surface

tablinum: the office or study of the head of the household

tribune: an elected official who led a plebeian assembly and was supposed to protect plebeian interests

FOR FURTHER READING

Bombarde, Odile, and Claude Moatti. *Living in Ancient Rome*. Ossining, New York: Young Discovery Library, 1987.

Brandt, Keith. *Ancient Rome*. Mahwah, New Jersey: Troll Associates, 1985.

Brooks, Polly Schoyer, and Nancy Zinsser Walworth. *When the World Was Rome*. Philadelphia: Lippincott, 1972.

Dillon, Ellis. *Rome Under the Emperors*. Nashville: Thomas Nelson, 1974.

Goor, Ron, and Nancy Goor. *Pompeii: Exploring a Roman Ghost Town*. New York: Thomas Y. Crowell, 1986.

Hicks, Peter. *The Romans*. New York: Thomson Learning, 1994.

James, Simon. *Ancient Rome*. New York: Alfred A. Knopf, 1990.

Leacroft, Helen, and Richard Leacroft. *The Buildings of Ancient Rome*. New York: William R. Scott, 1969.

Macaulay, David. *City: A Story of Roman Planning and Construction*. Boston: Houghton Mifflin, 1974.

Nardo, Don. *The Roman Empire*. San Diego: Lucent Books, 1994.

Rutland, Jonathan. *See Inside a Roman Town*. New York: Warwick Press, 1977.

Steele, Philip. *Food and Feasts in Ancient Rome*. New York: New Discovery Books, 1994.

Steffens, Bradley. *The Fall of the Roman Empire: Opposing Viewpoints*. San Diego: Greenhaven Press, 1994.

Windrow, Martin. *The Roman Legionary*. London: Franklin Watts, 1984.

BIBLIOGRAPHY

Grant, Michael. *The Founders of the Western World: A History of Greece and Rome*. New York: Charles Scribner's Sons, 1992.

Grant, Michael. *History of Rome*. New York: Charles Scribner's Sons, 1978.

Grant, Michael. *A Social History of Greece and Rome*. New York: Charles Scribner's Sons, 1992.

Grant, Michael. *The World of Rome*. Cleveland: World, 1960.

Hadas, Moses. *A History of Latin Literature*. New York: Columbia University Press, 1952.

Hamilton, Edith. *Mythology*. Boston: Little, Brown, 1942.

Hamilton, Edith. *The Roman Way*. New York: W. W. Norton, 1932.

Hooper, Finley. *Roman Realities*. Detroit: Wayne State University Press, 1979.

Johnston, Mary. *Roman Life*. Glenview, Illinois: Scott, Foresman, 1957.

Meyer, Marvin W., ed. *The Ancient Mysteries, a Sourcebook: Sacred Texts of the Mystery Religions of the Ancient Mediterranean World*. San Francisco: Harper & Row, 1987.

Parrinder, Geoffrey, ed. *World Religions: From Ancient History to the Present*. New York: Facts on File, 1983.

Perowne, Stewart. *Roman Mythology*. New York: Peter Bedrick Books, 1984.

Pomeroy, Sarah B. *Goddesses, Whores, Wives, and Slaves: Women in Classical Antiquity*. New York: Schocken Books, 1975.

INDEX

Page numbers for illustrations are in boldface

Aeneas (hero), **51**
Aeneid (Virgil), 20, 33–34
agriculture, 11, 40–41
amphitheaters, 22–25, **23, 24**
Antony, Mark, 15–16
Appian Way, the, 11, **11**
aqueducts, **21,** 21–22
architecture, 14–15, **20,** 20–24,
     30, 67, **67**
   Roman legacy in, 62, 64, 70,
     70
armies, **6,** 11–12, 17
art, 29–31, **30, 37, 63**
   in houses, **27,** 27–29, **28**
   Renaissance, 67, **68, 69**
Augustus, **15,** 34, **63**
   leadership of, **16,** 25
   power of, 15–16, 41–42

Bacchus (god), 45–46
barbarians, **19,** 62
baths, 22, **22**

Caesar, Julius, **6,** 14–15, 32,
     41–42
Carthage, wars with, 9–10
Ceres (goddess), 40, 44–45
children, 46, 52, 54–59, **55**
Christianity, 48–49, **62,** 63–64
Cicero (orator), **14,** 14–15, 45,
     66
   influence of, 31–32, 69–71
Cleopatra, 14, 16
Colosseum, 23, **23**
Constantine, emperor, 19, 49
Constantinople, 19, 62

education, 9, 56, **56,** 66–71
emperors, 16–19, 29–30,
     41–42, 60–63
Enlightenment, the, 71
entertainment, 22–25, **32,** 33

equites (class), 7, 12, 16
Etruscans, **7,** 21
Europe, Roman legacy in,
     62–65

family life, 36, 53–58, **50, 54**
festivals, 33, 37, 40, 46–48,
     56–57, 64
First Triumvirate, 14
Fortune and Fate, 40, 42–43, 48
Forum, 6, **8, 37,** 57

Germans, 17, **19,** 62
gladiators, 23–24
government, 6, 11–12, 16–19,
     51–52, 54, 60–61
   of republic, 7–8, 13–16
   Roman legacy in, 63–64, 71
Greeks, 9–10, 62, 67
   and art, 29, 31, 69
   and religion, 37, 41, 44–45

Hadrian, emperor, 17, **17, 20**
Hannibal (general), 9, **10**
Holy Roman Empire, 63
houses, 25–27, **26**

Isis (goddess), **43,** 48

Jews, 49
jobs, 54, 60–61
Judea, 13, 49
Juno (goddess), **39,** 39–40
Jupiter (god), **38,** 38–40

kings, Roman, 6–7

languages, 64–65
Lares (spirits), **36,** 36–37
laws, 9, 65–66
literature, 31–35, 67

marriages, 53–54, **54, 57,** 58
map, 18
men, 52, 55, 59
Minerva (goddess), 39–40
Mithras (god), 46, **47**
mosaics, 27–29, **28, 32**
mystery religions, 43–48, **43, 44–45**
myths, 37, **68, 69**

nations, conquered, 12–13, 49, 66
numina (spirits), 36–37, 40–41

Octavius. *See* Augustus
oratory, 31, 56
Ovid (poet), 34, **68, 69**

Pantheon (temple), **25, 62**
patricians (class), 6, 50–52
patriotism, 49–50
plays, 31, **32,** 33–35
plebeians (class), 7–9, 50–52
poetry, 32–34
Pompey (consul), 13–14, 49
popes, Catholic, 63, **64**
Punic Wars, 9–10

rebellions, 11–16, 49, 60
relief sculptures, 30, **30,** 31, **50**
religions, 19, 25, 36–49, **43**
    art of, 29, **37, 38, 39**
    mystery, 43–48, **44–45**
    Roman Catholic, 63–64, **64, 66**

worship of emperors, 41–42
Renaissance, 67–71
rituals, **43, 44–45,** 44–46
roads, 11, **11**
Roman empire, 16–19, 62
Roman republic, 7–14
Romulus, 6

Second Triumvirate, 15–16
Senate, 6–7, 14, 16, 52
    powers of, 12, 16
shrines, **36**
slaves, 11, 24–25, 33, **56,** 58–61, **61**
social classes, 6–9, 50–52, 56, 58
    struggles between, 11–12, 17–19
Social War, 12–13

temples, 25, **25**
Titus, emperor, 30, 49
Twelve Tables (laws), 9, 65

United States, 70–71

Vespasian, emperor, 42, 49
Vestal Virgins, **37,** 37–38, 53–54
Virgil (poet), 20, 33–34

wars, 9–14
women, 37–38, 44–46, 53–55, 59

About the Author

K athryn Hinds has always been fascinated by ancient cultures. As a child she dreamed of becoming an archaeologist or a writer. She grew up near Rochester, New York, then moved to New York City to study music and writing at Barnard College, where she took four semesters of Latin. She did graduate studies in comparative literature at the City University of New York. For several years she has worked as a freelance editor of children's books. She also writes poetry, which has been published in a number of magazines. Ms. Hinds now lives in the north Georgia mountains with her husband, their son, and three cats. Her other books in this series are *The Celts of Northern Europe* and *India's Gupta Dynasty*.